M000283664

Climb Every Mountain

Dr. Linda's Leadership Lessons

A Collection of My Favorite Books, Quotes & Poems

By Linda Edgar, DDS, MEd

Published by
Hybrid Global Publishing
333 E 14ᵗh Street
#3C
New York, NY 10003

Copyright © 2023 by Linda J. Edgar DDS, MEd

All rights reserved. No part of this book may be reproduced
or transmitted in any form or by any means, electronic or
mechanical, including photocopying, recording, or by any
information storage and retrieval system, without the written
permission of the Publisher, except where permitted by law.

Manufactured in the United States of America, or in the
United Kingdom when distributed elsewhere.

Edgar, Linda J.
Climb Every Mountain
    ISBN: 978-1-957013-19-0
    eBook: 978-1-957013-20-6
    LCCN: 2022904660

Cover design by: Joe Potter
Copyediting by: Virginia Earl
Interior design by: Suba Murugan
Author photo by: Saskia Potter

Dedication

To my husband,

Without you we would not have adopted our wonderful son, I would not have gone to dental school or become the leader I have had the good fortune to be. You have been my supporter and cheerleader for over 55 years.

Thank you… for being the:
"Wind Beneath My Wings"
A song by Jeff Silbar & Larry Henley

My husband, Bryan, and I at an
American Dental Association Dinner.

To my son,

You have been there to give us joy since we adopted you at three days. You have been my emotional support while my mom and dad were ill ...Your Dad and I are so proud of you — now a Captain for Alaska Airlines and an amazing father and husband.

To Judy,

Thank you for loving my son and supporting him and raising our two amazing granddaughters.

To Dr. Bruce Burton, my Campaign chair for the ADA Meeting,

I could not have won the ADA President Elect Election without your coaching and positive force ... Bruce also coaches leadership training .

To my granddaughters,

We love you so much and hope you will dream and know you can become whatever makes you the happiest. I hope you find your purpose and passion in life but most of all...
I hope you dance.

My two granddaughters dancing on the beach in Daytona.

Table of Contents

1	**My Leadership Story** *Climb Every Mountain*	**1**
	The shift	6
	Scary	10
	Stress galore	12
	Leadership	13
2	**My Favorite Quotes & Sayings**	**17**
	Leadership	13
	Effort	24
	Respect	24
	Appreciation	24
	Kindness	25
	Vision	26
	Quality	28
	Optimism	28
	Action	29
	Golden Rule	30
	Service	30
	Thank You	30
	Wisdom	41
	Leadership	41
	Diversity	42
	Possibilities	42

Change 42

Brilliance 43

Make It Happen 43

Cultivate 43

Winston Churchill Quotes 47

3 Leadership Development Books **51**

1. Now, Discover Your Strengths.......................... 51

2. The Difference Maker 53

3. The Power of Attitude................................. 57

4. Appreciation 58

5. Power of Nice.. 59

6. The Leadership Pill 60

7. You, Inc. 62

8. Exactly What to Say 63

9. Trusted Leader....................................... 65

10. The Speed of Trust 66

11. Blink.. 74

12. 21 Characteristics of a Leader 75

13. The Race 80

14. How Successful People Lead........................... 82

15. Crucial Conversations................................ 89

16. Influencer: The Power to Change Anything............. 93

17. Monday Morning Choices 93

18. Lincoln on Leadership................................ 94

19. How the Mighty Fall 96

20. Think Big, Act Small 98

21. Race for Relevance 99

22. Profiles in Courage 102

23. The Elephant and the Ant 102

24. The Eighth Habit 103

25. The Tipping Point 108

26. Beyond Emotional Intelligence 109

27. Quantum Leap Thinking 111

28. Leading Change 115

29. Inside the Nonprofit Boardroom 117

30. The 21 Irrefutable Laws of Leadership 118

31. 7 Measures of Success Getting to Yes 127

32. Anyway 130

33. The Art of Public Speaking 131

34. Selling 101 137

35. Raving Fans 140

4   Favorite Articles, Poems, Statements   143

1. The Bridge Builder 143

2. Persevere Boldly 144

3. Authenticity 144

4. Perseverance and Passion 145

5. Commitment 146

6. Courage and Confidence 147

7. Remember and Reconnect 148

8. Which Attitude will Win? The One You Feed 148

9. Article: Dealing With Difficult People 149

10. 101 Zen Stories 153

11. The Starfish Story 154

12. Poem: Risks 156

13. What is Class? 157

14. Communication 158

15. Speech Hints 158

16. Simplicity 159

17. The Man Who Wins Is the Man Who Thinks
    He Can 159

18. Don't Quit 160

19. Poem: Persistence 161

20. Rules for a Leader 161

21. Article: Daring to Trust Again 162

22. Persistence — My Story 163

Suggested Additional Leadership Books   164

Chapter 1

My Leadership Story
Climb Every Mountain

I was born in San Diego. My dad was a Coast Guard rescue pilot and my mother was a substitute teacher. When I was three months old my dad was transferred to Newfoundland and then to Miami, Washington, D.C., Virginia, the Philippines, back to Washington, D.C., to Puerto then to Port Angeles, in Washington State and finally back to San Diego where I was lucky enough to spend my senior year of high school as a brand new student at Claremont High with no friends.

I had met Bryan who has now been my husband for almost 50 years in Port Angeles as a sophomore in high school so having to transfer to San Diego in my senior year was especially devastating. My dad became an Admiral and CEO of the Coast Guard base in San Diego that same year in 1969.

One year later after graduation from high school, I decided to go to the University of Washington and study to go to medical school and become an OB-GYN. Bryan had his heart set on being a dentist, and we reunited when he transferred from Washington State University to the University of Washington so we could be together again.

My parents wanted us to wait until we graduated from college to get married so we decided I would teach until he finished dental school, and then it would be my turn to go back to school.

From 1973 to 1976, I taught junior high school to help put Bryan through dental school. I always had a goal of going to medical school and becoming an OB-GYN when Bryan finished his dental residency training, but at the age of 24 years old tragedy struck. After two and a half years of marriage we were in Bryan's senior year of dental school, and I experienced a ruptured tubal pregnancy and nearly bled to death on New Year's Eve. Nine months later during Bryan's first year of residency training the same tragedy hit — a second tubal pregnancy ruptured my remaining tube the night before Thanksgiving.

Suddenly my goal of becoming an OB-GYN was becoming less exciting. I was devastated because I always wanted to have children, and I thought Bryan might want to leave me and divorce me because I could not have children of our own. Regardless of my fears, I was very lucky and Bryan's love for me shone through when he wrote our name into the hospital's secret adoption list without me knowing. He did not tell me because he did not want me to get my hopes up.

Three months later... a miracle happened. A pregnant woman showed up in the hospital where my husband was doing his dental residency in Ft. Riley, Kansas, and wanted to give up her baby who was due to be born the next day. I cannot describe the feeling of going from the devastation at age 24 of not being able to have my own children to the possibility in 1977 of becoming an "instant mom" of a three-day-old baby.

Bryan and I basically decided overnight to go for it because her baby was to be born the next day. We thought, "when would we ever get another chance like this?" We got a lawyer and paid her $200 to draw up the papers. Every day we waited for the news of whether the baby was born.

We were so excited and couldn't believe after the devastating year we had had that this miracle could be happening for us. Would she change her mind? We went to garage sales and bought clothes, diapers and other baby supplies. I read Dr. Spock overnight, a "what to do when you have a baby book," and made a quilt. Our neighbors who had helped me during my depression after having the tubal pregnancies were so excited and happy for us. Everyone in the neighborhood had children and had advice for us.

Our "miracle baby" was born on April 29, 1977. We had to wait three days to pick him up at the hospital. A name? We did not have a name, but eventually it came to us. Bryan and I decided to call him David because of the David and Goliath story.

I tried to take David to work with me because we got David so quickly and Bryan was working in his residency program full time to finish up. The professor I was doing research for allowed me to do a split shift and work from 6:00 am - 10:00 am and go back and work a second shift from 6:00 p.m. - 10:00 p.m..

David had colic, however, and screamed much of the first month until we took him to the doctor and found out he was allergic to milk. We put him on a soy diet and that made a huge difference.

Needless to say, I got very little sleep the first few months. He was 8 pound 2 ounces when he was born, and once he started on soy he was growing off the charts and doubling his clothes size almost every month.

I have written a book called *Thank You for Giving Me David* to tell David's life story as a thank you to his biological mom.

Bryan's residency program was over when David was three months old and we moved back to Federal Way, Washington, so he could start his service in the Army at Ft. Riley. Although my intention was to stay at home and raise my son, a job opening fell in my lap. I was asked to teach math and science at Cascade a junior high in Auburn, Washington, and coach softball. As luck would have it, we had a wonderful woman named Doris in our neighborhood who babysat about four children and she did not have a baby. She took David in and helped him grow up. So David was always with other children and never felt like an only child.

I felt very broken after losing my babies and decided to start a running program in 1978 to prove my worth. I began adding more and more miles to my training increasing the distance I ran by 10%

a week and adding speed work and hills and 10K races. David and Bryan would come with me to my races and cheer me on. David often rode his bike beside me when I did my 20-mile training runs. Bryan was a good runner too and was very supportive of me. He watched David when I did my training runs at 5:30 am.

I was asked to move up to Auburn High School in 1980 where I coached track and cross-country racing and taught honors chemistry. To save training time and gas, I started running the eight miles to school, changed in the PE locker room, taught all day, ran with my students during cross-country practice and then ran the eight miles home. Four days a week I would put in 22 to 26 miles a day, run a few miles on Fridays to rest and do 10K races on Saturdays and/or Sundays.

To increase endurance, I often did back-to-back 10K races on Saturdays and Sundays and ran 10 more miles after the races to "warm down." The highest mileage I ever did in a week was 170 miles. I was not the most talented runner, but I was probably the hardest worker on the racing circuit. I knew if I did more miles and speed and hill workouts than my opponents that I could win the races. Part of me knew that I was just trying to fill the void left from losing the babies and winning was a way to perhaps help me fill that void.

My students and athletes loved the fact that their teacher was a runner and the state-mile and two-mile champions were on my track team.

For 10 years, from 1978-1988, I ran an average of 107 miles a week (over 52,000 miles), completed over 45 marathons with a best time of 2:42.58, set the record in the Seattle Marathon, and ran hundreds of 5K, 10K and half marathon races with best times of 17 minutes for the 5K, 35 minutes for the 10K and 1:17 for the half marathon.

I set a world record in the 50K (31 miles) of three hours and 21 minutes in 1983, and I qualified to run in the first Women's Marathon Trials in 1984 as one of about 250 women from across the nation who had run under a 2:51 marathon to qualify to run in the trials.

We had one year from May of 1983 until May of 1984 to run a marathon under the qualifying time of 2:51:16. I had already run that time about 15 times, but in March of 1983 I ran a race and ripped my Achilles tendon. I spent the rest of 1983 trying to qualify for the first ever Women's Olympic Trials Marathon.

In 1983, there were five women from the state of Washington, where I was from, who had a chance to do the qualifying time and run in the first Women's Marathon Trials so there was constant media pressure for us to qualify and represent our state.

As I had the fastest time in the marathon (2:42:58) in the state of Washington and had set a world record in the 50K (3:21), the pressure from the media for me to qualify to run this historic race was intense.

Every week leading up to the trials in May of 1984 there were articles in the newspapers asking, "Will she make it?" I kept trying to run marathons and qualify, but I spent a year racing and getting reinjured again and again and not healing because I was trying to race too soon.

Finally in March of 1984 just six weeks before the Olympic Marathon Trials' date, which was in May of 1984 in Olympia, Washington, I decided to try to qualify one last time. I ran the Emerald City Marathon and was on pace to do a 2:48 marathon, but I "hit the wall" at 20 miles.

I could hardly hold my head up when a woman came up and started running beside me. She was my angel. I knew if I could just keep going and get to the finish line of the marathon, my husband would catch me as I finished. Normally I was used to winning marathons, but in this race I was in 5th place — trying my hardest with a last chance to attain my goal of qualifying for the first-ever 1984 Women's Marathon Trials.

As I rounded the corner to the finish line, the huge crowd of spectators let out a roar of cheers as though I was the winner because many of them knew about my injuries and what I had been through to come back and keep trying over and over again to run below the qualifying time.

I was trying to each time I fell. Sure enough, Bryan was at the finish line when I collapsed with the final time reading, 2:50.59.

I had finally qualified for the first-ever Women's Marathon Trials with 17 seconds to spare. Unbelievable!

Linda after finishing
the First Woman's 1984 Olympic Trials.

The shift

I was 30 years old when I ran the Olympic Trials in 1984. That was a tough year of injuries and it took its toll. I continued to run marathons and win them for the next seven years. After running 45 marathons all over the country including many of the "BIG" ones like New York, Boston, San Diego Mission Bay and the San Francisco World Championships and many more I needed a new challenge and triathlons were beginning to become more popular. I was a good swimmer having competed in AAU swimming from the time I was eight years old, but I was terrible on the bike.

At age 37 I shifted to running the Ironman Triathlons, which is a 2.1-mile swim, 112-mile bike followed by a marathon (26.2 miles). I shifted to triathlons because I wanted a new challenge and I had been a good swimmer on swim teams growing up.

I had qualified to run in the World Championship Triathlon in Kona, Hawaii, in October of 1987 by winning my age group (30-35 years) in a shorter triathlon, but I decided to do another Ironman in Canada as training in August of that year.

The race had aid stations with bananas, and electrolyte drinks about every five miles because of the length of the triathlon, which took anywhere from 10 to 18 hours to complete. I had a good 2.2-mile swim and was out of the water in an hour and seven minutes. I was in 7th place over all women.

I got on my bike and took aid with my right hand at the top of a hill 30 miles into the race.

The race directors had failed to put anyone on the course to warn riders of the first set of railroad tracks, which was at the bottom of a steep hill and they had not covered them. I was racing downhill at about 30 plus miles an hour, and the man on the bike in front of me yelled,

"Railroad tracks."

I braked with my left hand because I had taken aid with my right hand at the aid station. I was trying to avoid the tracks. When you brake the bike with your left hand, it stops the front wheel suddenly. I was thrown off the bike and I crashed on the tracks, which split my helmet in two and bent my front wheel.

I got back on the bike and tried to continue about 30 more miles, but realized I was having trouble breathing. I also knew my wheel was bent and that I would not make it up and down the steep mountain passes in the bike race.

The race officials checked me out and said I should not continue. I had broken four ribs and so my "training race" ended up in a disaster. That race was on August 26, and the Ironman World Championships in Hawaii I had qualified for was in mid-October — just six weeks later after my accident.

I would not be able to train while I was healing, and I realized that my fate was inevitable. I had to give up my goal. I was very depressed as I watched my dream of competing in the World Ironman Championships on the Big Island of Hawaii vanish completely before my eyes.

I spent the next six weeks healing and watched the Ironman Championships I should have been in on TV. I felt lost because so much of who I thought I was — was tied up in my athletic success. I was pretty banged up from the crash where I landed on my head, split my helmet and could have died. I continued to train but decided to pursue other goals.

My son was 10 years old and I was 36 years old. I had been teaching high-school honors chemistry, and I was the head of my department. It was 1987 and computers in classrooms were becoming more common. I had gone to a National Institute of Health (NIH) course that summer on using computer simulations in chemistry labs, and I wanted to raise money to get computers in our high school and in my chemistry lab. Unfortunately, the head of the computer department wanted nothing to do with this idea. I think he just didn't want to make the effort to learn about something new.

I decided not to take no for an answer. I went to the school board and asked for a grant to get the computers. I received a $180,000 grant from this school board to bring computers into all the classrooms in my high school, including several in my chemistry lab.

The head of the computer department was not happy, and when the computers arrived — I didn't get any.

I had shown him the money could be granted and our department could progress into the future. However, he made sure I did not get the computers I had wanted for my chemistry lab to help the honors chemistry students. I am not sure why he treated me this way. Perhaps he was jealous that I actually accomplished something in my mind he should have been doing. Needless to say, I went to the superintendent and fixed the problem. The computers were sent to my chemistry lab for the students to use the following week.

I was also asked to teach computer simulations across the state, and I was coaching the top mile and two-mile runners in the state as well as our championship cross-country team.

My husband knew I was frustrated with the politics at the high school and the lack of funding for my honors chemistry vision for my students. As the only woman in the science department with an older department head who was not really interested in progressive change, it was difficult to improve and change curriculum. It was not an easy task to convince him to move into the future.

My athletic career had also taken a dive with the injuries from my crash in the Ironman race in Penticton, British Columbia, Canada. I was getting older and it was harder to train intensely enough to win races.

Meanwhile, Bryan decided to make a trip up to the dental school at the University of Washington and secretly get an application for me to apply to dental school, a dream I had put off when we adopted my son. We didn't really discuss what motivated him to surprise me. It's possible that he wanted me to go to dental school so he could have an "early retirement plan," but in retrospect I really think he realized I would be a good dentist and he wanted to help give me a push after everything I had been through.

The last thing I was thinking of was quitting teaching and going back to dental school the following year at the age of 37. Did dental schools even accept students that old? But I thought about it and we went ahead and filled out the long application with credits listed from the last 15 years, as well as my portfolio of races and speeches I had been asked to give as a runner and a coach. I figured, "What have I got to lose?"

The tragedy of my crash at the "practice Ironman" and broken ribs had opened my mind to trying something else — climbing another mountain — and applying to dental school.

We had three days to get the application back east so I could be considered for the University of Washington Dental School the following year. I only applied to that school because it was one of the best in the country, and I could not leave my son to go out-of-state to dental school. We put my application on a plane so it would reach the east coast the following day and beat the deadline.

I was busy teaching at the high school and had forgotten about the application. About a month after we sent the information in I got the call and was granted an interview. By some stroke of luck, the dentist who was interviewing me was very interested in my running portfolio because he was just beginning to train to run a marathon. The years of teaching impressed him as well as my Masters in Education and my grades had been good in college.

Then, a few weeks later I got the call that I had been accepted into the University of Washington Dental School and would start the following fall in 1988. It never occurred to me that I would get in. Now what do I do? I would live at home and commute the one to two hours to the school and would need to get more care for more hours for my son. I would be so old compared to my classmates. Would I fit in or be treated like an outsider?

Scary

My husband warned me against taking a leave of absence from teaching because he knew how tough dental school was, especially the first year. I did love teaching and cried my last day, knowing how very much I would miss my students and coaching. They tried to give me a congratulations going away party but I was too upset to go.

Dental school was definitely tough, and I had at least an hour to a two-hour drive each way to the University of Washington, which was north of Seattle. I lived at home in Federal Way, about 35 miles away from the university, so that I could care for my 11-year-old son while studying to get my degree. I was the only woman in my class of 54 students with a young son to raise. Bryan's mom, Laura, who had just retired from nursing, moved in to help me get David to his daily activities. This was a huge blessing because this gave David and Laura a chance to get to know each other better. We covered all of Laura's expenses, which was a help to her. David loved her grilled cheese sandwiches and she actually learned to drive in the big city. I think she felt she had a real purpose helping as she transitioned into retirement. I told her every day I could not have done this without her.

The first year I felt like quitting every week. We had 27 credits each quarter. The normal college load is 15 credits. The last class of the week was a waxing class where we had to form a perfect likeness of a tooth. During this waxing class, I was sitting alphabetically between a man who had done lab work for his father for eight years and another man who had designed jewelry. Not surprisingly, the instructors were not too impressed by my wax-ups compared to theirs.

I realized it had been 15 years since I had taken tests in college and my heart rate and blood pressure shot through the roof during our first test in histology. My pathology professor was the husband of a good friend of mine from college, which put a lot of pressure on me to do well.

One of the senior dental students at the University of Washington School of Dentistry had been in my science class when he was a seventh grader.

Talk about feeling out of place. But I didn't let anything stop me from moving forward. I studied hard every minute of every day, and with a lot of positive self-talk and encouragement from my husband, I did well.

In 1991, during my third year of dental school I got a call from my husband while I was in the middle of clinic. He was working in our private dental practice in Federal Way and also serving in the Army

Reserves. He never called me during the day so I knew the call was important. Something was up!

He said that he had been "called up to active duty" for the war called "Desert Storm." He was leaving the next day! Oh my — talk about a way to ruin your day!

I was in the middle of a practical exam on a patient, and after that call I wasn't myself. My mind was spinning, and I started to imagine all sorts of scenarios. Everything was closing in on me. Anxiety kicked in and I started shaking. My focus was gone and I could not finish the exam. All of a sudden, he would be gone — just like that — and there was nothing I could do and no telling for how long he would be away... Within seconds my mind was flooded with all sorts of questions. Would it be another Vietnam? He would be on Army pay. What would we do with the dental practice? Too many questions to get answers to... and we didn't even have a will. Our lives changed within seconds.

Stress galore

He left for the war and I did my best to handle dental school, raise our 13-year-old son, manage the practice and our new associate. There was so much uncertainty about when Bryan would return from Desert Storm. Would the practice survive? How would we manage our bills and dental school costs on a military salary? Thank goodness the war was over in nine months, and he was back in a year. What a relief!

I graduated a year later, passed my dental board exams and finally joined the practice. I immediately got involved in setting up continuing education programs and organizing study clubs for the Washington Academy of General Dentistry (WAGD), which had not been real active. I also acted as the WAGD executive director and joined the WAGD board. My son was 15 years old and had grown nine inches during my senior year of dental school. He was six feet eight inches and very involved in basketball.

Meanwhile, Bryan was also involved in organized dentistry serving on the board of the Seattle King County Dental Society and the Washington State Dental Association (WSDA) where he was on the Budget and Finance Committee and later became treasurer.

He started the Investment Committee, which he is chair of, and later became president and now chair of the Investment Committee and of the Regulatory Committee that represents the WSDA at the Washington State Board of Dentistry. He has also served six years on the national Academy of General Dentistry as the speaker of the house and has also served at the National American Dental Association (ADA) as an elected delegate, one of 485, for over 20 years.

After serving on the WAGD Board from 1992 as Continuing Education Chair, treasurer and then president elect and president in 2005, I decided to run for Board of Trustees of the Academy of General Dentistry (AGD), which is the second largest dental association in the country with close to 40,000 members. This person represents Region XI, which is comprised of five states (Alaska, Montana, Idaho, Oregon and Washington). It was a close race but I won. There were only a few women on this 28 member-board at the time.

After serving for two years as a trustee, the national AGD Secretary position came open and I ran and won. I had also been serving concurrently on the Seattle King County Dental Society (SKCDS) board and was elected president of SKCDS that same year. I served two terms. I was also elected to serve as an ADA delegate starting in 2005. It was during my four years as AGD Secretary that I felt the need to learn more about leadership.

Leadership

I started reading and summarizing leadership books and seeking out quotes because I was asked to speak at several events representing our organization. I summarized many of the books and started collecting quotes, stories and poems and shared these with other leaders. I felt unprepared in my leadership role and sought out guidance absorbing all I could.

I also gave these leadership book summaries to the other 20 AGD trustees and AGD officers to help them with speeches and in general to help them with the leadership roles they were asked to perform. After serving two year-terms twice as secretary, I was encouraged to run for AGD national president and won. I was only the second woman to hold the presidency of the AGD in 60 years. In addition, I also had the honor to serve on the Washington State Dental Association Board.

In 2017, my husband encouraged me to run for the position of national American Dental Association (ADA) Trustee for my District XI, which covered Alaska, Idaho, Montana, Oregon and Washington dentists.

This ADA board represents dentists across the entire country and develops policy for dentistry in the US and also contributes to dental policy around the world. It was scary but I ran against two men and won. There are only two to four women on the ADA Board of 23 people at any one time. Our ADA trustee term is four years long.

Once again my husband was "the wind beneath my wings," and after almost 50 years of marriage he is still my rock and has helped give me the confidence to rise up and take another leadership role.

When I was in dental school in the 90s we only had 11 women in a class of 54 students. Now many dental schools are admitting and graduating, often at the top of their classes, over 50% women.

So, the time is now to show that women too can lead, can inspire and can move our organizations forward. Women lead to make a difference and if my example will help a future woman leader, I will try to help her shine.

This is my background and my leadership story in a nutshell. What follows are excerpts and summaries from several of the leadership books I have read, as well as poems and a list of my favorite quotes that I have used in speeches throughout my career to inspire others. I want to share this information with other leaders so that they too can use it as a reference tool for their speeches and/or talks, and hopefully find either a quote or book that will guide them and inspire them in their leadership journey, as well as in their personal lives.

I call this my handbook of "leadership lessons" — A book to motivate you to "Climb every mountain" and "Get up each time you fall."

This is my gift to you to possibly help your leadership story and journey be easier.

I have learned an incredible amount from these books. I hope this collection will help you as well in your personal and professional growth and that you will be able to inspire and guide others along the way.

We can realize out of every tragedy can come a triumph if we face things with the right attitude.

Linda finishing the Penticton Ironman at age 45 in 12 hours and thirty-six minutes.

Chapter 2

My Favorite Quotes & Sayings

Leadership

The Essence of Leadership
By Mac Anderson

A true leader has the confidence to stand alone, the courage to make tough decisions and the compassion to listen to the needs of others. They do not set out to be a leader, but become one by the quality of their actions and integrity of their intent. In the end, leaders are much like eagles, they don't flock. You find them one at a time.

Unless you try to do something beyond what you have already mastered you will never grow.

— *Ralph Waldo Emerson*

The power of the human spirit — Climb every mountain and believe without a doubt that you can succeed.

— *Anonymous*

Teamwork is the fuel that allows common people to attain uncommon results.

— *Andrew Carnegie*

The leader's job is to look into the future and see the organization, not as it is, but as it could be.

—Jack Welch

Problems can become opportunities when the right people come together.

—Robert Redford

Adversity reveals character.

—James Lane Allen

The best way to predict the future is to create it.

—Abraham Lincoln

You will always miss 100% of the shots you do not take.

—Wayne Gretzky

Excellence is never an accident. It is always the result of high intention, sincere effort, intelligent direction, skillful execution and the vision to see obstacles as opportunities.

—Aristotle

Never doubt that blending your talents with those of others can change the world.

— Eleanor Roosevelt

Never doubt that a small group of thoughtful, committed citizens can change the world; indeed, it's the only thing that ever has.

— Margaret Mead

Leadership is about taking charge and influencing others to follow your vision. It's about going against the odds and accepting responsibility for the outcomes along the way.

—Robin Crow

If you want to lead the orchestra, you must turn your back to the crowd.

— *Islwyn Jeneins*

True leadership must be for the benefit of the followers, not the enrichment of the leaders.

—*Robert Townsend*

Real leaders are ordinary people with extraordinary determination.

—*John Seaman Garns*

It is a fact that in the right formation, the lifting power of many wings can achieve twice the distance of any bird flying alone. As each goose flaps its wings it creates an "uplift" for the bird that follows. By flying in a "V" formation, the whole flock adds 71% greater flying range than if 1 bird flew alone."

— *Lessons From the Geese*

by Robert McNeish

Do not go where the path may lead, go instead where there is no path and leave a trail.

—*Ralph Waldo Emerson*

Photo credit: Steve LePenske

Live daringly, boldly, fearlessly. Taste the relish to be found in competition —in having to put forth the best within you to match the deeds of risk-taking, hard-working competitors.

—*Henry J. Kaiser*

Accept the challenges, so that you may feel the exhilaration of victory.

—*George S. Patton*

Wisdom is knowing the right path to take. Integrity is taking it.

—*M. H. McKee*

One hundred years from now, it will not matter what my bank account was, the sort of house I lived in, or the kind of car I drove. But the world may be different because I was important in the life of a boy.

— *Forest E. Witcraft*

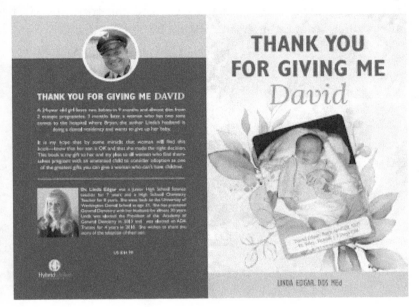

David, my son, whom we adopted
at age three days old.

Greatness is not in where we stand but in what direction we are moving. We must sail sometimes with the wind and sometimes against it — but sail we must and not drift or lie at anchor.

— *Oliver Wendell Holmes Jr.*

True leaders are not those who strive to be first but those who are first to strive and who give their all for the success of the team. True leaders are first to see the need, envision the plan and empower the team for action. By the strength of the leader's commitment — the power of the team is unleashed.

—*Anonymous*

The block of granite, which was an obstacle in the pathway of the weak, became a stepping-stone in the pathway of the strong.

—*Thomas Carlyle*

In the confrontation between the river and the rock, the river always wins — not through strength but by perseverance.

—*H. Jackson Brown*

A goal without a plan is just a wish.

—*Antoine de Saint-Exupéry*

You can climb every mountain presented to you in your life if you start with baby steps — and consistently move forward toward your dream every day!

—*Linda Edgar*

Never let a good crisis go to waste.

— *Winston Churchill*

"A little less conversation, a little more action, please"

—*Elvis Presley, Recording*

"A Little Less Conversation" (A song by Billy Strange & Mac Davis)

I continue to say "I would rather get three things done" than "Talk about doing 100 things."

—*Linda Edgar*

During my days as a marathon runner I would often have top female runners come up to me after a race — a 10K or marathon that I won — and say, "I could beat you if I ran as many miles as you do every week." My reply was always, "Then just do it."

After testifying in front of the ADA House of Delegates about a heated topic, a very tall (six foot three inches) delegate came up to me. He poked me in the chest with his finger and said, "You are not going to win this one." To which I replied, "Watch me."

If your work is helping others and you are doing the right things for the right reasons, remember you are as strong and as smart as anyone.

My dad was a two-star admiral in the Coast Guard and my uncle was a three-star general in the army and they put their pants on one leg at a time just like you and I do. If you work hard and know your stuff you are as good and worthy to be heard as anyone — no matter what gender or what race you are.

—*Linda Edgar*

Leadership is action, not position.

— *Donald H. McGannon*

All of us have an inherent need for a clear sense of purpose in life. People are never happy unless they move toward accomplishing something that is really important to them.

—*Linda Edgar*

Entering the flow of abundance begins when exceeding expectations become a way of life.

—*Robin Crow*

Nature has proclaimed that difficulty should precede every work of excellence.

— *Anonymous*

Effort

At 211 degrees F, water is hot but at 212 it boils.
One extra degree in life separates the good from the great.

— Sam Parker

Respect

Diversity is being asked to the party. Inclusion is being asked "to dance."

—Verna Myers

What people crave most is attention and respect.

—Linda Edgar

"Always do right. This will gratify some people and astonish the rest."

—Mark Twain

Don't ever stand on a pedestal. People don't want to know how good you are.
They want to know how good they can be.

—Linda Edgar

Half effort does not produce half results, it produces no results.

—Hamilton Holt

Appreciation

You never know when a moment and a few sincere words can have an impact on a life

—Zig Ziglar

How is what you do every day making someone's life better?
Appreciation is a wonderful thing. It makes what is excellent in others belong to us as well.

—Voltaire

You never know who may be silently hurting who you might save by a kind act or a kind word.

— Robin Williams

To who might you give an unexpected gift of appreciation today?
There are two things that people want more than almost anything — recognition and praise.

—Mary Kay Ash

Kindness

If you have a choice between being right and being kind, choose being kind.

—Dr. Wayne Dye

Seize the day to be kind and make a difference in someone's life.

—Linda Edgar

One of the best feelings in life is to shine a light upon another.

— Marianne Williamson

Share yourself from your heart genuinely. Appreciation only works if it is authentic.
Your simple act of kindness will be remembered by the person forever.

—Linda Edgar

I expect to pass through this world but once. Any good therefore that I can do, or any kindness

I can show to any fellow-creature, let me do it now. Let me not defer or neglect it for I shall not pass this way again.

—Stephen Grellet

Take time to listen — really listen to others …
Take time to care and "pay kindness forward" every day.
If everyone did this, just think of the world we could have

—Linda Edgar

I expect to pass through this life but once.
If therefore, there can be any kindness I can show,
or any good thing I can do for any fellow human being,
Let me do it now, for I shall not return this way again.

—William Penn

Life's most persistent and urgent question is "What are you doing for others?"

—Dr. Martin Luther King

History will have to record the greatest tragedy of this period was not the strident clamor of bad people, but the appalling silence of good people.

—Dr. Martin Luther King

If you can't feed a hundred people, then feed just one

— Mother Teresa

In this life we cannot do great things. We can only do small things with great love.

—Mother Teresa

Vision

The executives of the future will be rated by their ability to anticipate problems rather than meet them as they come.

— John Maxwell

Be proactive instead of reactive.

—*Stephen Covey*

Advanced planning is like taking a deep breath before the plunge.

— *J. R. R. Tolkien*

The will to win is worthless, if you don't have the will to prepare.

— *Thane Yost*

The formula for failure is to try to please everyone.

— *Herbert Bayard Swope*

Great leaders have enthusiasm and relentless optimism and persistence.

Great leaders take full responsibility for what goes wrong.

No excuse is the best excuse.

A leader offers an example of courage and sacrifice!

If something goes wrong, the leader is the first one to take the responsibility.

—*Linda Edgar*

I will not make age an issue of this campaign. I am not going to exploit for political purposes my opponent's youth and inexperience.

— *Ronald Reagan.*

A simple idea can make a powerful impact.

Dream big dreams, but never forget realistic, short-term goals are the baby steps that ultimately make one giant footprint.

—*Linda Edgar*

Focus on the critical few not the insignificant many.

Less is usually more.

— *Chris Bello*

The highest achievement of a leader is winning the respect and trust of your team.

— *John C. Maxwell*

Quality

In the race for quality there is no finish line.

—*David Kearns*

Quality is never an accident. It is the result of high intention, sincere effort, intelligent direction and skillful execution.

—*William Foster*

Be frugal in your management of member's
money, but generous in your service!
The most critical issue is serving the member and making every moment and every membership dollar count.
Make your brand stand for something.

—*Linda Edgar*

Optimism

Optimism is the faith that leads to achievement.

—*Hellen Keller*

Embrace Humor, Hope & Optimism
Whether you think you can or you think you can't, you are probably right.

—*Henry Ford*

It is not the things you get but the hearts you touch that determine your success in life.

— *Maya Angelou*

It matters not, how much we own, the cars, the house,
the cash. What matters most is how we live and love
and how we spend our dash.

— Linda Miles & Mac Anderson

Action

Imperfect action is better than perfect inaction.

—Harry Truman

"A little less conversation, a little more action, please"

—Elvis Presley, Recording

"A Little Less Conversation" (A song by Billy Strange & Mac Davis)

It is a funny thing about life.
If you refuse to accept anything but the best,
You very often get it.

—W. Somerset Maugham

Courage does not always roar.
Sometimes it is the quiet voice at the end of
the day that says, "I will try again tomorrow."

—Mary Anne Radmacher

Some men see things as they are and say, why.
I dream things that never were and say, why not.

— George Bernard Shaw

The person who constantly says, "It can't be done," isn't noticing the people doing it.

—Anonymous

Where there is a will there is a way.

—George Herbert

Eliminate the word "impossible" from your vocabulary
—Linda Edgar

If we wait for the perfect answer the world will pass us by.
— Jack Welch

The Golden Rule

Do unto others as you would have them, "Do unto you."
If you teach a child, the Golden Rule you will have
left them an estate of incalculable value.
— Ilene Cooper

Resolve to be tender with the young, compassionate with the aged,
sympathetic with the striving, and tolerant of the weak and the
wrong.
Sometime in life you will have been all of these.
— Lloyd Shearer

Service

Service is the very purpose of life.
It is the rent we pay for being on this planet.
— Marion Wright Edelman

We can never help another without helping ourselves.
— Ralph Waldo Emerson

Thank You

How often as a leader, how many times a day, a week,
a month, do we pass up the opportunity to thank those
people in our lives, or businesses and our organizations
who are "doing the heavy lifting to help us be successful,"

who are in the shadows doing the work, who are
"packing our parachutes" so we have a safe landing?

— *Charles Plumb*

I can do two months on a good compliment.

— *Mark Twain*

The things that get rewarded and appreciated get done!

—*Micheal LeBoeuf*

Be bold with audacious goals.

—*Brad Borkan*

Whenever you see a successful business, someone
has made courageous decisions.

— *Peter F Drucker*

One of my favorites
Care more than others think is wise;
Risk more than others think is safe;
Dream more than others think is practical;
Expect more than others think is possible

— *Claude T. Bissell*

Love does not make the world go around
Love is what makes the ride worthwhile.

— *Franklin P. Jones*

God grant me the serenity to accept the things
I cannot change, the courage to change the things I can
and the wisdom to know the difference.

— *Alcoholics Anonymous & Reinhold Niebuhr*

Forgiveness is the key that unlocks the handcuffs of hate.

— *William Ward*

Dream as if you will live forever.
Live as if you would die today.

— *James Dean*

It's never too late to call an old friend.

— *Jeanie Miley*

Do the Impossible
I only hope that we never lose sight of one thing — that it was all started by a mouse.

— *Walt Disney*

The only place success comes before work is in the dictionary.

— *Vince Lombardi*

The greatest accomplishment in life is not in never
falling but in rising after you fall.

— *Vince Lombardi*

Those who dare to fail miserably can achieve greatly.

— *John F. Kennedy*

We must become the change we want to see in the world.

— *Mahatma Gandhi*

An eye for an eye ends up making the whole world blind.

— *Louis Fischer, The Life of Mahatma Gandhi*

It is not the critic who counts; not the man who points out how
the strong man stumbles, or where the doer of deeds could have
done them better. The credit belongs to the man who is actually

in the arena, whose face is marred by dust and sweat and blood; who strives valiantly; who errs, who comes short again and again, because there is no effort without error and shortcoming; but who does actually strive to do the deeds; who knows great enthusiasm, the great devotions; who spends himself in a worthy cause; who at the best knows in the end the triumph of high achievement, and who at the worst, if he fails, at least fails while daring greatly, so that his place shall never be with those cold and timid souls who neither know victory nor defeat.

— *Theodore Roosevelt*

Miscellaneous Quotes

The truly wise person is colorblind.

Consistent kindness can accomplish much.

As the sun makes ice melt, kindness causes misunderstanding, mistrust and hostility

to evaporate.

— *Albert Schweitzer*

Leadership is example.

Example is not the main thing that influences others. It is the only thing.

The only people who are truly happy are those

who have found how to serve.

The purpose of human life is to serve, show compassion

and the will to help others.

–*Albert Schweitzer*

Your boss is the customer (or member).

— *Sam Walton*

You can't build a reputation on what you are going to do.

— *Henry Ford*

Differentiate yourself. Care deeply.

—*Anonymous*

Courage is fear holding on a minute longer.
Moral courage is the most valuable and usually the most absent characteristic.

— *George S. Patton Jr.*

The best prize life has to offer is the courage to work hard at something worth doing.
You can choose to push people down or pull people up.
Speak softly and carry a big stick.

— *Theodore Roosevelt*

It takes a lifetime to build a relationship and only a few seconds of harsh words to destroy it.

— *Warren Buffet*

Your candle loses nothing when it lights another.

— *James Keller*

You have not lived until you do something today for someone who can never repay you.

— *John Bunyan*

Courage does not always roar. Sometimes it is the quiet voice at the end of the day saying, "I will try again tomorrow."

— *Mary Anne Radmacher*

A goal without a plan is simply a wish.

—*Antoine de Saint-Exupery*

Beautiful light is born of darkness, so the faith that springs from conflict is often the strongest and the best.

— *Ross Turnbull*

Service is the rent we pay for being. It is the very purpose of life and not something you do in your spare time.

— *Marian Wright Edelman*

Collaborate

Be the light that others can come to with their ideas, visions and dreams. Never doubt that blending your talents with those of others can change the world.

—Margaret Mead

Never doubt that a small group of thoughtful,
committed citizens can change the world; indeed, it's the only thing that ever has.

— Margaret Mead

Perseverance

In the confrontation between the stream and the rock, the stream always wins, not through strength but by perseverance.

— H. Jackson Brown Jr.

The rock that is an obstacle in the path of one person may be a stepping stone for another.

— Thomas Carlyle

Change

If you are not riding a wave of change, you will find yourself beneath it.

— Karen Martin

Quality

Countless unseen details are often the only difference between mediocre and magnificent.

— Mukul Khatiwara

Life is what happens while you are busy making other plans.

— John Lennon

The most difficult thing is the decision to act.

— *Amelia Earhart*

The best time to plant a tree is 20 years ago. The second best is today.

—*Chinese Proverb*

Criticism

To avoid criticism, do nothing, say nothing, be nothing.

— *Elbert Hubbard*

All that is necessary for the triumph of evil is that good men do nothing.

— *Edmund Burke*

Few things can help an individual more than to place responsibility on them and trust them.

— *Booker T. Washington*

Life is not measured by the number of breaths we take, but by the moments that take our breath away.

— *Maya Angelou*

Business goes where it wants to but it stays where it is appreciated.

—*Anonymous*

If you want people to listen to you, you must first be willing to see things from their point of view.

—*Roger Fisher*

Presence

People with presence have an unselfish attitude that causes them to put other people first. They possess a positive attitude that prompts them to look for and focus on what is right instead of what is wrong. They possess an unshakable confidence.

—Anonymous

If you wait until you can do everything for everybody, instead of doing something for somebody, you'll end up not doing anything for anybody.

— Malcom Bane

Create special moments and honor people when they least expect it. Express your gratitude in front of others.

—Linda Edgar

To be human is to mess up. To connect you must fess up. Be accountable and deliver on your promises. There is strength in saying, "I am sorry."

—Nancy Marshall

When you make a commitment you create hope.

—John C. Maxwell

Integrity is doing what you say you will do.

—John C. Maxwell

When we choose not to focus on what is missing from our lives but are grateful for the abundance that's present ... we experience heaven on earth.
Both abundance and lack exist simultaneously in our lives, as parallel realities. It is always our conscious choice which secret garden we will tend ... when we choose not to focus on what is missing from our lives but are grateful for the abundance that's present — love, health, family, friends, work, the joys of nature and personal pursuits that bring us pleasure — the wasteland of illusion falls away and we experience Heaven on earth.

—Sarah Ban Breathnach

It is a funny thing about life. If you refuse to accept anything but the best — you very often get it.

— *W. Somerset Maugham*

It is not the things you get but the hearts you touch that determine your success in life.

— *Maya Angelou*

It is amazing what one can accomplish when you don't know what you can't do.

—*Jim Davis*

It is amazing what you can accomplish when you don't care who gets the credit.

— *Harry Truman*

Adversity does not build character, it reveals it.

— *James Lane Allen*

Entering the flow of abundance begins when exceeding expectations become a way of life.

— *Robin Crowe*

Advanced planning is like taking a deep breath before the plunge.

— *J. R. R. Tolkien*

Focus on the critical few not the insignificant many.

— *Pareto Principle*

I expect to pass through this world but once. Any good therefore that I can do, or any kindness
I can show to any fellow-creature, let me do it now. Let me not defer or neglect it for I shall not pass this way again.

— *Stephen Grellet*

Sometimes you just need to let go of the picture
of what you thought life would be like and learn to
find joy in the story you are actually living.

—Rachel Marie Martin

It's not the strongest of the species nor the smartest
of the species that survive, but the ones most adaptable
to change.

— Charles Darwin

Whatever you can do to dream you can, begin it;
Boldness has genius, power and magic in it.

— Johann Wolfgang von Goethe, Translated by John Anster

In the end, we only regret the chances we did not take!

— Lewis Carroll

Folks are usually about as happy as they make up their minds to be.

—Abraham Lincoln

It always seems impossible until it's done.

— Nelson Mandela

The only thing we have to fear is fear itself.

— Franklin Delano Roosevelt

In any given moment we have two options: to step forward
into growth, or step back into safety.

— Abraham Maslow

Only those who risk going too far can possibly find out
how far they can go.

— T.S. Elliot

It's not what you get into; it's how you get out of it.

— Miles Davis

If one moves confidently in the direction of their dreams
and endeavors to live the life they have imagined, they will
meet a success unexpected in common hours.

—Henry David Thoreau

It is in our darkest moments that we must focus to see the light.

— Aristotle

May you always be courageous, stand upright and be strong.
May you stay forever young.

— Bob Dylan

If your dream only includes you, it's too small.

—Ava Duvernay

A good exercise for the heart is to bend down and help another up.

— John Holmes

A bubbling brook would lose its song if you removed all the rocks.

— Wallace Stegner

People will give, join and contribute if they feel they are making
a difference.

— Linda Edgar

It's amazing what one can accomplish when one doesn't know what
one can't do.

—Jim Davis

"Great organizations focus on service adding value and empowering
others.

Look at the brutal facts of your organization — are you doing this?"
— *Good to Great: Why Some Companies Make The Leap and Others Don't*

> — *By Jim Collins*

You don't throw a whole life away just because it is banged up a little.

> — *Tom Smith*

Courage is the strength to be different from the crowd.

> —*Brené Brown*

A wave of love will wash away a footprint of hatred.

> —*Anonymous*

Wisdom

Knowledge that moves from the head into the heart becomes wisdom.
Wisdom is the beneficial use of knowledge
Wisdom is information and knowledge impregnated with
a higher purpose.

> —*Anonymous*

Leadership

The future of leadership will increasingly require creative interdisciplinary and possibly international collaborations.

> —*Anonymous*

Be a servant leader. Listen to the desires of others and work to empower their passion.

> —*Bethany Van Benschoten*

We cannot solve today's problems at the same level of knowledge and wisdom that we had when we created them.

—*Albert Einstein*

Spend time to prepare "the ground," so that when we do plant we have given it every chance to succeed.
Persistence + Preparation + Planing = Propulsion

—*Linda Edgar*

Aspirations without action are worthless.

— *Helen Keller*

Diversity

The mountains need valleys
The water needs the sand
And we all need each other,
To lend a helping hand
We're the colors of the rainbow, we're the stars up in the sky.
No two of us are quite the same.
For it takes a world of difference to make a difference in our world.

—*Partial lyrics of "A World of Difference"*
Artist- Bemis

Possibilities

Whatever the mind can believe, it can achieve.

— *Napoleon Hill*

Change

If you are not riding the wave of change, you will find yourself beneath it.

— *Karen Martin*

Brilliance

When a collection of brilliant minds, hearts and talents come together, expect a miracle.

—Anonymous

Make it happen

Greatness is not where we stand but in what direction we are moving.

— Oliver Wendell Holmes

I respect any person who can heal a heart he didn't break and raise a child he didn't make.

The two saddest words are "IF only"

Our lives begin and end the day we become silent about things that matter.

— Martin Luther King Jr.

When everything seems to be going against you, remember that the airplane takes off against the wind, not with it.

— Henry Ford

The will to win is worthless if you don't have the will to prepare.

—Thane Yost

Cultivate

Pull the weeds — otherwise the garden will not grow.
Do good for others.
Hold others up and make them shine.
Collaborate with others to do good.
Listen and learn from each other.

— Linda Edgar

C4 — Caring, Connections, Create, Commitment

— Linda Edgar

Recognition and praise is more powerful than money or sex.

—Mary Kay Ash

Education is the most powerful weapon you can use to
save the world.

—Nelson Mandela

A house divided on itself cannot stand.

— Abraham Lincoln

An eye for an eye makes the whole world blind.

— Mahatma Gandhi

The word commitment means to ignite action.

—Anonymous

It is better to take a single small step than just " talk about" running
a marathon.

— Linda Edgar

Leading by example is one of the most important qualities
of leadership.

—Stephen Covey

We wildly underestimate the power of the tiniest personal touch.
How many lives will you touch along the way?

— Tom Peters

You can't steal second base with your foot on first base.

— Fredrick B. Willcox

The greatest gap in life is the one between "I should" and "I did."
— *Anonymous*

Three words are essential in connecting with others: brevity, levity and repetition. Three tenets of a great speech.
— *John C. Maxwell*

Be the bridge of action. Problems become opportunities and tragedies become triumphs.
— *Linda Edgar*

And where does the power come from to see the race to its end? From within.
—*Eric Liddell, Chariots of Fire*

It is better to set a goal and miss it than never set a goal and accomplish it.
—*Anonymous*

Behold the turtle. He makes progress only when he sticks his neck out.
— *James Bryant Conant*

The race is not always to the swift but to those who keep on running.
— *Jan Rutherford*

Courage is the finest of human qualities because it guarantees all others.
—*Winston Churchill*

Well done is better than well said.
— *Benjamin Franklin*

Kind words can be short and easy to speak, but their echoes are endless.

— *Mother Teresa*

Life's most persistent and urgent question is "What are you doing for others?"

—*Martin Luther King Jr.*

A good name like goodwill happens by many actions and is lost by one.

— *By Warren Buffett*

Things that matter most must never be at the mercy of things that matter least.

—*John Wolfgang von Goethe*

Our greatest glory is not in never falling, but in rising each time you fall.

— *Oliver Smith*

You cannot build a reputation on what you are going to do.

— *Henry Ford*

You can't live a perfect day without doing something for someone who can never repay you.

— *John Wooden*

Focus on the critical few, not the insignificant many.

— *Anonymous*

Before we "build a better mousetrap," first we have to find out
if there are mice out there.
Build a better mouse trap and the world will beat a path to your door.

— *Ralph Waldo Emerson*

Wisdom is knowing the right path to take. Integrity is taking it.

— *Julie Benezet*

One of my favorite quotes is "85% of all statistics are made up on the spot."

— *David Mitchell*

Silent gratitude isn't much good to anyone.

— *Gertrude Stein*

The test of inspiration is action.

— *Elvis Presley*

Winston Churchill Quotes

You will never reach your destination if you stop and throw stones at every dog that barks.

Fear is a reaction.
Courage is a decision.

A nation that forgets its past has no future.

The positive thinker sees the invisible, feels the intangible and achieves the impossible.

Success consists of going from failure to failure without loss of enthusiasm.

A pessimist sees the difficulty in every opportunity; an optimist sees opportunity in every difficulty.

One man with conviction will overwhelm a hundred who only have opinions.

However beautiful the strategy, you should occasionally look at the results.

We contend that for a nation to tax itself into prosperity is like a man standing in a bucket and trying to lift himself up by the handle.

I'd rather argue against a hundred idiots, than have one agree with me.

Life is fraught with opportunities to keep your mouth shut.

A lie gets half way around the world before the truth has a chance to get its pants on.

An appeaser is one who feeds a crocodile, hoping it will eat him last.

The most valuable of all talents is never using two words when one will do.

The harder I work, the luckier I get. Do unto others as you would have them do unto you.

It takes a lifetime to build a relationship and only a few seconds of harsh words to destroy it.

A little rebellion now and then is a good thing.

Climb Every Mountain

Mount Rainier

Chapter 3

Leadership Development Books

1. NOW, Discover Your Strengths

By Marcus Buckingham & Donald O. Clifton, PhD

Strengths Finder Profile

This book has an online test, which comes up with your five most powerful strengths.

When I first read it, I did not trust the test so I bought it two more times and took the test a total of three times. The results of my five greatest strengths were close to the same with achiever, learner, connectedness, developer, maximizer as the ones "my test" revealed.

NOW, Discover Your Strengths emphasizes the importance of concentrating on your strengths instead of your weaknesses. It talks about the value of developing teams around the strengths that people have.

The following are the 34 strengths the authors talk about:

Achiever	Arranger
Activator	Belief
Adaptability	Command
Analytical	Communication

Competition	Individualization
Connectedness	Input
Context	Intellection
Deliberative	Learner
Developer	Maximizer
Discipline	Positivity
Empathy	Relator
Fairness	Responsibility
Focus	Restorative
Futuristic	Self-assurance
Harmony	Significance
Ideation	Strategic
Inclusiveness	Woo

Take the test and find out what is right about you. Find out what your strengths are.

Most organizations are inefficient at capitalizing on the strengths of their employees.

Each person is unique in their strengths.

The greatest room for growth is in improving their strengths not their weaknesses.

Build a strengths-based organization. The real tragedy in life is that we fail to use the strengths we have. Discover your strengths and organize your life so these strengths can be applied.

The three most important principles in building a strong life:

1. You must be able to do it consistently.
2. You must derive satisfaction from it. It energizes you.
3. You don't need to be "well-rounded."

You will excel only by maximizing your strengths not by trying to fix your weaknesses.

First understand how to distinguish your natural talents from the things you can learn.

To develop a strength in any activity, requires certain natural talents.

- **Talents** are your naturally occurring thoughts, feelings or behaviors.
  The <u>Strength Finder Profile test</u> measures these.
- **Knowledge** is the facts and lessons learned.
- **Skills** are the steps of an activity.

You can buy this book and take the online test in the back to determine where your talents lie.

These three things: talents, knowledge and skills — combine to create your strengths.

- Your **talents** are innate but **knowledge** and **skills** can be acquired.
- Hunt for areas of your greatest potential.
- You need factual knowledge and life experience.
- Always "set the stage." Tell your audience who they are watching and why, or they will tune out.

2. The Difference Maker: Making Your Attitude Your Greatest Asset

By John C. Maxwell

1. Focus on "people skills" and "The Golden Rule."
   Have a positive attitude of kindness.
   Always try to see things from the customer or member's point of view.

Teddy Roosevelt once said, "The most important single ingredient in the formula for success is knowing how to get along with people."

2.   Impossible is just a big word thrown around by "small" people who find it easier to live in a world they have been given than to explore how to change your world for the better.

3.   In order to have progress, we must change the way we think.

Five attitude obstacles:

- Discouragement
- Change
- Problems
- Fears
- Failures

Overcoming obstacles is a necessary part of life. Learn to embrace this instead of fear it. When faced with a challenge in my dental practice, like a patient that had been unreasonable, I would say to my staff:

"In the 'big picture' of life this is a very little thing.
Recognize what is wrong and focus on the solution.
None of us are perfect."

If you look at the most successful people in life, most of them share one thing in common — persistence.

Robin Williams once said, "Remember everyone you come in contact with may be fighting some kind of battle."

- Be a "lifter"
- Be an encourager
- Make things happen.

Fear will hold you back, but the only thing to really fear is fear itself. When you want something you have never had, you must do things you have never done.

As a distance runner, I started out running 5Ks, then 10Ks at a nine-minute pace, but I wasn't satisfied with that. I wanted to see if I could do better. I read articles and running books and found out if you just add about 10% more miles a week and gradually add faster running, hill running and interval training that you could improve your times.

I started running in 1978 at the age of 27 to lose weight. I was doing about 20 miles a week and running about a 58-minute 10K. After trying other things, I gradually added miles and speed, nutrition and weight loss to my running protocol. Over the next three years I built up my mileage to over 100 miles a week. I found out that every pound of extra weight you carry adds a minute to a marathon and every five extra pounds adds a minute to your 10K.

I took copious notes and studied what workouts allowed me to improve. I discovered that if I added a six-minute mile at the end of a 20-mile training run for the marathon that soon I could run that marathon at a six-minute per mile pace.

In three years, I ran a marathon in 2:42:58, which is about a 6:10 pace per mile.

Yes, I was sore and yes it was tough to push myself, but with persistence and consistency I grew from a mediocre runner to one who was winning races and making money doing it.

Tom Peters, an American writer, once said, "Don't rock the boat … Sink it and start over." We cannot allow ourselves to be paralyzed by the fear of change. No matter how far you have traveled on the wrong road don't be afraid to turn back.

PROBLEMS

"Waiting for ideal conditions is rarely an option." Sometimes you have to "fix things" in the eye of the storm. You can choose how you respond to problems — you can let them make you weak or you can let them make you strong. One of the most commonalities between successful people is that they all overcame problems and adversity

— physical, emotional and financial problems. This prompted them to achieve.

Anticipated problems can be an opportunity. The first step in solving a problem is to begin. When JFK was asked how he became a war hero he said, "Someone sunk my boat."

Try to find the three best solutions to any problem. Focus on the mission and move on.

FEAR

The only thing we have to fear is fear itself.

— *Franklin Delano Roosevelt*

ROOSEVELT

At age 39 Roosevelt contracted polio. He overcame his fear of fire and falling.

The only way to escape from the prison of fear is action. Fear keeps us from reaching our potential.

When a leader is ruled by fear, he or she puts a lid on the people that follow them.

The emotion you feed is the one that will dominate in your life.

I lived through this. Therefore, I can take the next thing that comes my way.

Sometimes you just have to jump off the cliff and build your wings on the way down.

FAILURE

There are three types of people : the "wills" the "won'ts" and the "can'ts."

The first type accomplish everything. The second type oppose everything. The third type fails at everything.

Life means risk. You will miss every shot you do not take.

— *Wayne Gretzky*

The two saddest words in the human vocabulary are "if only." Change these words to "next time."

Replace the word failure with "learning experiences." Sometimes you win and sometimes you lose. Don't take your successes or your failures too seriously.

Never, never, never give up!

The difference maker in your life can help you make the difference in the lives of others.

3. The Power of Attitude

By Mac Anderson

Tomorrow will be a better day.
Every day I constantly choose to maintain the right attitude.
Keep difficulties from defeating you.
You will "rise up" if you choose to.
Help others believe in themselves, have hope and work positively to overcome problems and add value to others.
Take time to "thank someone" who has made a difference in your life.
Success should be judged by the seeds you sow not the "harvest you reap."

— *The Power of Attitude*[1]
by Mac Anderson

Attitude is everything.
Destiny is not a matter of chance. It is a matter of choice.
Wherever you go, go with all your heart.
Great was never accomplished without enthusiasm.

— *Ralph Waldo Emerson*

[1] Anderson, Mac. *The Power of Attitude*. (United States, Thomas Nelson, 2004).

When we choose to not to focus on what is missing
from our lives but are grateful for the abundance
that is present, we experience heaven on earth.

— *Sara Ban Breathnach*

A journey of a thousand miles begins with a single step.

— *Deng Ming-Dao*

Winning is not a sometime thing; it's an all-time thing.
You don't win once in a while.
You don't do things right once in a while.
You do them right all the time.
Winning is a habit.
Unfortunately so is losing.

— *Vince Lombardi*

4. Appreciation

By Mac Anderson

Appreciation: Everyone wants it and needs it.
There is always an opportunity for kindness.
It doesn't have to be something big — just something
that says to the other person, "You are worthwhile,
you are full of promise" or after a failure,
"You will rise again another day!"

The happiness of life is made up of minute fractions — the
little, soon forgotten charities of
a kiss, or a smile, a kind look or heartfelt compliment.
Go ahead – make someone's day –
when you do it will make your day too.

— *Samuel Taylor Coleridge*

5. The Power of Nice: How to Conquer the Business World with Kindness

By Linda Kaplan Thaler & Robin Koval

Jay Leno once said, "Doing good things will improve your life.
We live in a society where common courtesy is so uncommon.
Success is won not with pitchforks and spears but with flowers and chocolates.
Being nice is placing other people's needs on the same level or above your own." **Principles of Nice**

1. Positive impressions are like seeds. If you spread them around, the entire garden flourishes.
2. People change – It pays to be nice to your students.

> I taught junior high science in the 70s and met a young student who wanted to be a dentist. He knew my husband was a dentist and asked me to come in after school to tutor him on the frog dissection. So I did. In 1988, I decided to go to dental school at the University of Washington, and guess who was a senior in dental school the year I started as a freshman?

3. Nice must be authentic from your heart — not forced.
4. The real measure of a person's character is how you treat the janitor, cab driver or waitress, or someone who can do absolutely nothing for you.
5. Help others shine. Shed the me versus you mentality.
6. Share the credit.

> It's amazing what you can accomplish when you don't care who gets the credit!
>
> — *Harry Truman*

7. Share the ownership of an idea and create a collaborative community.

8. Embrace diversity and include people who have differences of opinion.
9. Boost the morale of people around you, and see how great it makes you feel.

Picture of Linda (freshman) and Todd (senior) in dental school.

6. The Leadership Pill: The Missing Ingredient in Motivating People Today

By Ken Blanchard & Mark Muchnick

"If you could have anything you wanted in a leader what would you wish for?"

- Trust. Walk their talk.
- Integrity. Do what you say you are going to do.
- Partnership. Help leaders work, learn and grow together.
- Leaders get to know their people beyond their job titles.
- Affirmation. Making people feel valued.

- People are more apt to trust and respect you when what you say and do are one and the same.
- Communicate. Sharing the big picture puts everyone on the same page.

Praise is most effective when it is specific, sincere and given as soon as possible after the desired behavior occurs. Praise is the easiest way to let people know they are appreciated.

Leading people is the opposite of trying to control them. Leadership is not what happens when you are there — it's what happens when you are not there.

When you turn customers or members into raving fans, they become part of your sales force.

Effective leaders get both commitment and results.

Profit is the applause you get for taking care of your customers or members.

Good Leaders Value Their Team

Affirmation is letting your people know they are valued.

As a dentist, we rely on our assistants to help our patients be comfortable.

During a procedure, I would try every day to catch my assistants doing something exceptional, and I would complement them in front of the patient.

If they made a mistake, I would talk to them in private to let them know we were growing toward exceptional service.

Most of my dental assistants stayed with me throughout my entire career because they felt valued, and I was interested in their private lives and challenges too. The same thing is true for your patients. Take the time to talk to them and genuinely care about them, their families and their lives.

Call them at home the night of an appointment to be sure they are doing okay.

If you do this, you will be exceptional and patients will also stay with you your whole career.

People don't care how much you know until they know how much you care.

— Maya Angelo

But, be real. Show them that you genuinely care.

Mentor your new staff to help give them a chance to be exceptional.

You are not the only one capable of running a meeting.

Give your staff shared responsibilities and allow them to shine.

Recharge

Be sensitive to burn out in your team if you are pushing too hard.

Take a break to celebrate your "wins." This helps recharge everyone's batteries.

7. You, Inc.: The Art of Selling Yourself

By Beckwith & Christine Clifford

Attitude matters. Attitude sells.

The most critical thing is being positive.

> People "buy" people with integrity because they do what they say they are going to do.
>
> — *You, Inc.: The Art of Selling Yourself*[2]
> *by Beckwith & Christine Clifford*

> A jack of all trades is a master of none, but oftentimes better than a master of none
>
> — *Viktor Vicsek*

- People trust specialists.
- If you try to appeal to thousands, you will appeal to no one.
  - Find out what your inquirer needs and focus on that need.
  - The best leaders continually search out "future stars."
  - The visual overwhelms the verbal.

[2] Clifford Beckwith, Christine., Beckwith, Harry. You, Inc.: The Art of Selling Yourself. (United States: Grand Central Publishing, 2007).

8. Exactly What to Say: The Magic Words for Influence and Impact

By Phil M. Jones

The Magic Words for Influence and Impact

When presenting a new idea to a group ask the question, **"Do you consider yourself open minded?"**

A conversation becomes a debate because the person you are speaking to thinks they know more than you do. The best way to overcome this is to question the facts or knowledge on which the other person's opinion was formed. Their opinion may not have been based on facts.

Ask, **"What do you know about ...?** This will help soften the conversation.

The real world tells us a person will work harder to avoid losing. Are decisions made from logic or emotion? Usually, they're made from emotion first.

People make decisions on what "feels right."

How would you feel if ...?
For a decision to come true, you must first at least imagine yourself doing it.

Just imagine the impact this would have.
(This creates a picture in the other person's mind.)

When would be a good time to ...?
(This prompts the other person to assume there will be a good time, and keeps control of the conversation.) **So what do you like about it?**

I am guessing you haven't gotten around to ... .

Swap **"Do you have any questions?"** for **"What questions do you have for me?"**

Use **"What is the best number to contact you at?"** is better than **"Can I have your phone number?"**

People want to think they made the final decision.

"As I see it, you have three options. Of these three options, which one would be the easiest for you?" (Leave for last the one you want them to choose.)

There are two types of people in this world.
Those who leach off others and let them pay their way and those who take professional responsibility for their profession and pay their dues.

I bet you are a bit like me.
Conditioning from childhood: If you ..., then (this will happen).
Use in high-stressed situations. Puts people at ease: Don't worry...

Instead of telling the person what "they should do," share what "most people would do" in this situation ...

Turning around negative energy, spins a negative into a positive by labeling.
The good news is that you already know this is not working so why not try something new?

People who give excuses: **Respond with "That's great! You have just found another way that does not work."**

To move a conversation toward action say: **"What happens next is** ... (Don't ask them what they would like to do.)

Maintain control in a conversation by asking the question: **"What makes you say that?"**
Ask the other person to explain their point of view.

"**Before you make your mind up about …, let's look at the facts.**"
Removing barriers: "**If I can …, then will you?**"

Getting the other person to reach a little higher: "**Would every six months work for you?**"

Offering a down sell: "**Just one more thing …**"

"Can you do me a small favor?"

"Just out of curiosity, what specifically do you need more time to think about?"

What kind of results? Answer: Good ones.

There is no such thing as being too grateful or too appreciative.

How to be believed: Admit a weakness.
The heart of a great relationship is trust.
Those who speak badly of others will speak badly of you.

Handling adversity with grace impresses people for life.

9. Trusted Leader: 8 Pillars That Drive Results

By David Horsager

1. **Clarity It is important to show the person HOW to take action.**
   A mission statement should inspire action every day
2. **Compassion**
   Every team member should know how much you care about them. You need to really see people and understand their needs — people could rely on others.
3. **Character**
   What you do when no one is watching.

4. **Competency**
   An extreme desire to learn and improve at everything. Have a mentoring system.
5. **Commitment**
6. **Connection and camaraderie**
7. **Contribution**
8. **Consistency**

10. The Speed of Trust: The One Thing That Changes Everything

By Steven M. R. Covey

> For every thousand people hacking at the leaves of evil, there is one striking at the roots.
>
> *—Henry David Thoreau*

The focus is on optimization through developing an ethical character, transparent motivation, and superb competence in producing sustained, superior results.

The heart and soul of all success is trust.

How do we transform a culture of low trust into a culture of high trust?

Speed to market has become the ultimate competitive edge.
Low trust — It causes friction whether it be from unethical behavior or by ethical or incompetent behavior. Low trust creates hidden agendas, politics, interpersonal and interdepartmental conflict, winning versus losing, thinking, defensive and protective communication — all of which reduce the speed of trust.

Low trust slows everything down — every decision, every communication and every relationship.

The greatest trust building key is results.

Trust impacts us 24/7. It impacts every relationship.
Trust is the key leadership competency in the new global economy.

Jack Welch, former chairman and CEO of General Electric one said, "If you are not fast, you are dead."

Trust — You know it when you feel it.
When you trust people, you have confidence in them.

Mahatma Gandhi once said, "The moment there is suspicion about a person's motives — everything they do is tainted."

- It is important to be candid and transparent and get the tough issues out on the table.

- Seek first to understand their concerns and create a feeling of hope and excitement.

- The real test, however, is the follow through.

- Integrity is doing what you say you are going to do.

- One of the fastest ways to restore trust is to make and keep commitments.

- High Trust = High Speed and Low Cost.

- The world is changing really fast.

- Big will not beat small anymore.

- It will be the fast beating the slow.

- Trust is a function of two things: character and competence.

- People trust people who make things happen.

- Do the right thing and get the right things done.

5 Waves of Trust

1. Credibility
2. Consistent behavior
3. Alignment
4. Reputation
5. Contribution

Credibility — It's determined by integrity, intent, capabilities and results. Make a clear commitment to act with integrity.

Integrity is the root system/Intent is the trunk/Capabilities are the branches/Results are the fruit.

Albert Einstein once said, "Whoever is careless with the truth in small matters is not likely to be trusted in important matters." Mahatma Gandhi said, "What a person thinks, feels, says and does are all the same."

Humility — *Good to Great: Why Some Companies Make the Leap... and Others Don't* by Jim Collins describes the best leaders to be a blend of humility and professional will.

A humble person is more concerned about what is right than in being right and...

- About acting on good ideas rather than having good ideas
- About embracing new truths rather than defending outdated positions.
- About Building the team rather than exalting themselves
- About recognizing contributions rather than being recognized.

Courage — Do the right thing even when it is hard. Stand for something.

Intent — The trustee acts in the best interest of the person or organization they represent.

Wayne Dyer said, "The measure of your life is not what you accumulate, but in what you give away."

Capabilities — When left unattended, knowledge and skill like all assets depreciate in value surprisingly quickly.

The complacent company is a dead company. Success today requires the agility and drive to constantly rethink, reinvigorate, react and reinvent.

—Bill Gates Jr.

RESULTS

It is no use saying, "We are doing our best". You have got to succeed in doing what is necessary.

—Winston Churchill

Consistent Behavior

What you do has far greater impact than what you say.

It takes 20 years to build a reputation and five minutes to ruin it.

—Warren Buffet

- Talk straight while demonstrating respect.
- Leaders with humility believe standing firmly for principle in the face of opposition.
- They recognize that they do not stand-alone but need others.

13. BEHAVIORS

1. **Talk Straight**
   Make commitments and take a stand.
   —Straightforward talk and honesty is vital.
   —Describe things as they are with no spin.

2. **Demonstrate Respect**
   —The biggest secret to success is how you treat others.
   —Show kindness in the little things and don't fake it.

3. **Create Transparency**
   —It is about being open, genuine and real.
   —What you see is what you get.
   —Err on the side of disclosure.

4. **Right Wrongs**
   —Admit mistakes — never cover them up.
   —Do what you can to correct a mistake and a little more.
   —Don't let pride get in the way of doing the right thing.

5. **Show Loyalty**
   —Give credit to the person who has done the work.
   —Give credit abundantly.
   —Speak about others as though they are present.
   —Never badmouth others behind their back.

6. **Deliver Results**
   —Establish a track record of results.
   —Get the right things done.
   —Make things happen.
   —Be on time and within budget.
   —Don't overpromise and under-deliver.

7. **Get Better**
   —The illiterate of the twenty-first century will not be those who
   cannot read, but those who cannot learn, unlearn and relearn.

—People stop learning because they are less willing to risk failure.
—Seek feedback and implement it.
—Learn from failures.

8. **Confront Reality**
    —Interact with openness and respect.
    —Addressing reality takes courage, responsibility, awareness and respect.
    —Confront brutal facts head-on.
    —Address the tough stuff directly.
    —Don't skirt the real issues.

9. **Clarify Expectations**
    —All conflict is a result of violated expectations.
    —Create shared vision and agreement about what is done upfront.
    —The number one reason for unethical actions is unreasonable expectations.
    —Make it happen by quantifying: What is the result?
    —By when, by whom and at what cost?

10. **Practice Accountability**
    —Set expectations first. Then do what you say you are going to do.
    —Victory has a hundred fathers and defeat is an orphan. —John F. Kennedy.

11. **Listen First**
    —If there is any great secret in life, it is the ability to put yourself in the other person's place and see things from their point of view.
    —Really listen and seek to understand another person's thoughts, feelings, experience and point of view.
    —Do this before you try to diagnose, influence or prescribe.
    —The opposite is to try to get out your agenda without listening to anyone else. This is self-focused, ego driven and does not build trust.

12. **Keep Commitments**
    —This is the quickest way to build trust.
    —Do what you said you were going to do.
    —Always deliver.
    —Never make a promise you can't follow through.

13. **Extend Trust**
    —There is nothing that motivates or inspires people more than being trusted to do a good job.

Market Trust
- Deals with external stakeholder.
- Reputation is the hardest one to regain.
- You can destroy a reputation almost instantly.
- You earn reputation by trying to do hard things well.

Societal Trust
- Every kind of peaceful cooperation among people is primarily based on trust.
- Individuals seeking to make a difference.

Men build too many walls and not enough bridges.

—*Sir Isaac Newton*

> # Get outside of yourself and "see" situations from the other person's standpoint.

The book *Good to Great* by Jim Collins states, "The practices of the best companies is to gather data, analyze it and confront the brutal facts to find the 'Inconvenient Truths.'"

ORGANIZATIONAL TRUST

Low Trust Organization

- People manipulate or distort facts
- People withhold or hoard information
- Getting the credit is very important
- People spin the truth to their advantage
- New ideas are openly resisted and stifled
- Mistakes are covered up
- Most people are involved in a blame game
- There is an abundance of "water cooler" talk
- There are numerous meetings after meetings
- There are many "undiscussables"
- People tend to overpromise and under-deliver
- There are a lot of violated expectations for which people try to make excuses
- People pretend bad things are not happening or are in denial
- The energy level is low
- People often feel unproductive tension.

High Trust Organizations

- Information is shared openly
- Mistakes are tolerated and encouraged as a way of learning
- The culture is innovative and creative
- People are loyal to those who are absent
- People talk straight and confront real issues
- There is real communication and real collaboration
- People share credit abundantly
- There are few meetings after meetings
- Transparency is a practiced value
- People are candid and authentic
- There is a high degree of accountability
- There is vitality and energy
- People feel a positive momentum.

Low-trust organizations have redundancy. Everything is checked and double checked.

- Multiple layers of bureaucracy
- Politics to gain power
- Disengagement of people
- Turnover
- Fraud

High trust organizations

- Have increased value. Things are done more efficiently
- Accelerated growth and enhanced growth
- Improved collaboration
- Stronger partnerships
- Better execution of strategy
- Heightened loyalty

11. Blink: The Power of Thinking Without Thinking

By Malcolm Gladwell

Blink people make very sophisticated decisions on the spur of the moment.

Blink is like a "gut check" if it does not "feel" like the right decision, it may not be.

People who are asked to write down their thoughts will be 30% less creative with problem solving. Paralysis through analysis. When they get so caught up in mechanics, they don't look at the problem connectively. Extra information can be more than useless — it can be harmful.

Real successful decision-making relies on a balance between deliberate and instinctive thinking.

The second lesson in decision-making is frugality.
Too many choices make people less likely to buy.

The process draws you in, you digest everything and try to synthesize the whole. If you get caught up in the production of information you can drown in the data.

There can be as much value in the "blink" of the eye as in months of rational analysis.

12. 21 Characteristics of a Leader:

By John C. Maxwell

Character, Charisma, Commitment, Communication, Competence, Courage, Discernment, Focus, Generosity, Initiative, Listening, Passion, Positive Attitude, Problem Solving, Relationships, Responsibility, Security, Self-Discipline, Servanthood, Teachability, Vision

Charisma
"I have yet to find the man, however exalted his station, who did not do better work and put forth greater effort under a spirit of approval than under a spirit of criticism."

— *Charles Schwab*

Focus on others. Help others, love others, share resources to make others better.

Commitment
The only real measure of commitment is action.
Commitment — means you press on.

Communication

A leader must be able to transfer knowledge with a sense of urgency — take something complicated and make it simple. They connect, they are clear and they focus on people.

They make decisions easily and delegate. Give the listener something to feel, to remember and to do. Inspire, motivate, guide, direct and listen.

Competence

Accomplish more than what is expected. Good enough is never enough. Continue to improve.

Courage

Is the quality that guarantees all others.
Doing what you are afraid to do.
Be willing to take risks.
Standing up and doing the right thing in the face of adversity.

Sometimes you just have to "Jump off the cliff and build your wings on the way down."

— *Rad Bradbury*

"You gain strength, courage and confidence by every experience in which you really stop to look fear in the face. You are able to say to yourself, 'I have lived through this horror. I can take the next thing that comes along.' ... You must do the thing you think you cannot do."

—*You Learn By Living: Eleven Keys for
a More Fulfilling Life³* by Eleanor Roosevelt

---

³ Roosevelt, Eleanor. *You learn by living*. (United States: Westminster Press, 1983), 11.

Discernment

Smart leaders believe only half of what they hear. Discerning leaders know which half to believe.

The first rule of holes: When you find yourself in one, stop digging. Never ignore a gut feeling but never feel that is enough.

"I think there is a world market for about 5 computers," said Thomas Watson, chairman of IBM, 1943.

Focus

People who are great at what they do can "cut out the noise and concentrate."

Prioritize

If you chase two rabbits, you will lose them both.

—Leonard Nimoy

Generosity

A candle loses nothing by lighting another candle.

—James Keller

The measure of a true leader is not in the number of people who serve them but in the number of people they serve. Look for ways to add value to another.

Initiative

Success is connected to action.

- Leaders know what they want and act on it.
- Leaders take more risks.
- Leaders make mistakes.

Even the right decision is the wrong decision if made too late.

— Lee Iaccoca

Listening

To connect with your heart, use your ears.

The ear of the leader must ring with the voices of the people.

Listen and act.

—Woodrow Wilson

Passion with a positive attitude.

Essential to be an effective leader.

Your people are a mirror of your attitude.

Problem Solving

The measure of success is not whether you're having a tough problem but if it is the same problem you had last year.

- Anticipate the problem
- Accept the truth
- See the big picture
- Handle one problem at a time

Relationships

People don't care how much you know until they know how much you care.

Responsibility

If you won't carry the ball, you can't lead the team. A leader can give up anything except final responsibility.

—John C. Maxwell

Security

Celebrate victories other than your own.

Self discipline
Work and prepare, challenge your excuses, stay focused.

No reward until the job is done.

Servant Leader
- Puts others ahead of their own agenda
- Possesses the confidence to serve
- Initiates service to others
- Is not position conscious
- Serves out of love
- Listens to others and risks for their benefit
- Performs small acts of kindness
- Walks slowly through the crowd and takes time
- to know others
- Acts to serve others.

Teachability
It's what you learn after you know it all that counts.

—John Wooden

Be a lifelong learner. Learn as if you will live forever.

Vision
You can seize only what you can see.

The future belongs to those who can see possibilities before they happen.
True vision goes beyond what one person can accomplish.
A true vision unites others.

The vision has to be really important and nearly impossible — that is what draws out the winner in people.

Discontentment with the status quo is a great catalyst for vision.

—John C. Maxwell

If you can see it and believe it, you can accomplish it.

—Napoleon Hill

13. The Race: Life's Greatest Lesson

By Dee Groberg

Quit! Give Up! You're beaten! They shout at me and plead.
There's just too much against you now
This time you can't succeed.
And as I start to hang my head in front of failure's face,
My downward fall is broken by
the memory of a race.

And hope refills my weakened will
As I recall that scene
For Just the thought of that short race
Rejuvenates my being.

A children's race — young boys, young men —
How I remember well
Excitement sure, but also fear;
It wasn't hard to tell.

They all lined up so full of hope;
Each thought to win the race.
Or tie for first, or if not that,
At least take second place.

And fathers watched from off the side
Each cheering for his son.
And each boy hoped to show his dad
That he would be the one.

The whistle blew and off they went
Young hearts and hopes afire.
To win and be the hero there
Was each young boy's desire

……..

But as they speed down the field
Across a shallow dip
The little boy who thought to win
Lost his step and slipped

……..

Sad embarrassed he only wished
To disappear somehow

But as he fell his dad stood up,
And showed his anxious face,
Which to the boy so clearly said,
"Get up and win the race."

……..

He slipped and fell again
Defeat He lay there silently
A tear dropped from his eye
There's no sense running anymore
Three strikes: I'm out! Why try?

……..

Bet then he thought about his Dad
Who soon he'd have to face
Get up and win the race

……..

He resolved that win or lose at least he wouldn't quit!

……..

But when the fallen youngster
Crossed the line last place,
The crowd gave him the greater cheer,
For finishing the race

And even though he came in last,
With head bowed low, unproud,
You would have thought he' d won the race
To listen to the crowd.

To me, you won, his father said,

You rose each time you fell.

14. How Successful People Lead: Taking Your Influence to the Next Level

By John C. Maxwell

Everything rises and falls on leadership.

—John C. Maxwell

5 LEVELS OF LEADERSHIP

Level 1
People follow you because they have to because of your position.
These people may be bosses but they are never leaders. Their people will only do what is required of them. Position does not require ability and effort to achieve.

Level 2
People follow you because they want to.
This level is based on relationships. When you treat people as individuals with value you develop trust and begin to have influence. The environment is positive. You cannot lead people without liking them.

Level 3
People follow you because of what you have done for the organization.
When leaders get things done they gain influence and credibility. Work gets done and goals are achieved. Here leaders become a change agent.

Level 4
People follow you because of what you have done for them.
Leaders become great because of their ability to empower others. Leaders reproduce themselves. These leaders change the lives of people they lead.

Level 5
People follow you because of who you are and what you represent.
This is the pinnacle. This level requires effort, skill and a high level of talent.
Good leaders do not lead everyone the same way because everyone is different.

Think about how long it takes to build a relationship.
If you do something to lose trust with that person, the relationship can become permanently broken in the blink of an eye.
At this level you create generations of leaders.
To stay at this level you must constantly grow, learn and improve.
To succeed as a leader you must help others succeed

Leaders who do the greatest harm to an organization are the ones who think they have
"arrived."
To build an environment of trust you must do the right thing for the right reasons.
An invitation to lead people is an invitation to make a difference.
Leadership of any kind is about working with people.
You must develop relationships to get people who get things done.
It takes no time at all to let others know you value them.

Shift your focus from "me" to "we."

What you must give others:

"I hear what you say."
"I see what you say."
"I feel what you say."

You have my undivided attention. I value who you are and what you say.

Nothing lifts a person like being respected and valued by others.
In times of difficulty relationships are a shelter.
In times of opportunity, relationships are a launching pad.

Trust is required for people to create, share, question, attempt and risk.
You must have trust for teamwork to work.

Conflict is part of the process. It allows us to look at hard truths, see people's flaws, face reality and do it in a spirit of grace and truth.
Leaders don't avoid problems —they solve them.
As long as people have a pulse you will be dealing with messy and difficult situations.
Treat others as you would like to be treated. Become the chief encourager.
Care balanced with candor creates developing relationships.

Level 3 leaders lead by example
Leadership is defined by what a person does with and for others.
Know that every person adds value.
Leaders describe the vision and what the target is.
Teams don't win unless the leader is totally committed.

Walk the Talk
VALUES * INTEGRITY * HONESTY *
TRUST * COMMITMENT *
RESPONSIBILITY * RESPECT

Trust, not technology, is the issue of the decade.

—*Tom Peters*

TRUST IS EVERYTHING

If you are doing leadership alone, you are doing it wrong!
Trust is a very fragile thing. It can take a lifetime to earn it and just a moment to have it destroyed.
Leaders can lose sight of reality.
Trust is the central currency of business.
Identify the team's values, personal passions, strengths and areas of improvement.

Compassion: We want our members and our team to feel truly valued and appreciated.

Your fastest opportunity to build trust is in a crisis.

When you have a crisis you ask two questions:

1. What can I control? Narrow your focus to a single priority. The goal in a crisis is to get through it, not get everything done. This will keep the group from getting distracted and make sure things get done completely.
2. What can I do right now?

Another hallmark of a crisis is that things usually happen rapidly. You need to maintain agility

Character: A sense of right and wrong. It is what you do when no one is looking.

A Lack of trust is your single biggest expense.

- When trust goes down everything moves in the wrong direction.
- Time, Money, Customer Loyalty, Retention, Reputation
- Take every chance you can to build trust.
- Your team needs to feel safe and empowered to provide exceptional service.
- They need to feel safe to talk about what is going right and what is going wrong.
- Develop collaborative conversation.
- Camaraderie, support and results that are exceptional — results we can be proud of.
- Freely sharing success methods

CONTRIBUTION

It is important to feel like what you do matters and makes a difference to someone else.
Think about what you can contribute rather than what you can get.

Action is what leads to results

- Ask yourself, "What is my single priority today?"
- What is your Difference Making Action (DMA)?
- Act on the most important task first.
- Don't let the things that matter the least get in the way of the things that matter the most.
- Create a welcoming space where everyone's voice can be heard and people are valued for who they are.

COMMITMENT

If you haven't identified a way to action, you have not gone deep enough.
This is what is missing in so much diversity, inclusion and equity work.

- Recognize we all make mistakes — listen with humility and realize we are all in this together.
- It all starts with listening and ends with action.
- Engage with all perspectives — especially those that are different from yours.
- Building equity into a company takes being intentional — you can't walk away even if it is uncomfortable.
- Diversity without trust makes problems worse.
- The hardest thing about leading is having to see what you need to see.

- If you build trust genuinely, your likeability factor will go up.
- The way to amplify a marketing message is to increase the audience's trust in the message!

> # Authentic long-term success can only be achieved in a culture of trust.

In a culture of trust people will work together, be creative, share information and become more productive. They demonstrate loyalty to the team and are willing to go the extra mile to ensure success.

With extra trust members will tell others how great your company or organization is.

The only way to increase engagement is to increase trust.

- So how do we increase trust?
- Confront your reality
- Look at the root causes of trust issues—Not doing what you say you are going to do —-No Integrity
- Create a common language
- Apply trust tools

Make people feel valued and listened to

Every day I try to do the best job I can to make my staff and my patients feel valued. People love to be listened to and made to think their thoughts and feelings are valued and that you hear them.

Take action

You cannot discover new oceans unless
you have the courage to lose sight for the shore.

— *Andre Gide*

Take action on bold audacious ideas.
Don't' be afraid to go out on a limb.
That is wear the fruit is.

— *Bob Ross*

Trust and respect serve as the constant
unconscious heartbeats of an authentic
leader.

Few things can help an individual more than placing responsibility
on them and letting them know you trust them. Be a level five
leader.

15. Crucial Conversations: Tools for Talking When the Stakes are High

By Joseph Grenny, Kerry Patterson, Ron McMillan & Al Switzler

What makes a conversation crucial is getting the truth out on the
table when emotions are running strong. The ability to talk openly
about high-stakes emotional and controversial topics is crucial.
Sometimes you just need to throw out the meeting agenda and talk
about the "elephant" in the room.

Hold each other accountable through face-to-face conversation at
all levels.

Be wary when people hold back and don't contribute or go silent.
Argue honestly and respectfully.

Share your views even if they are controversial.
Make it safe to share.
The more information the better the decision.

When people aren't involved in the decision, they are rarely committed.
Opinion leaders speak up and maintain respect.

Mutual Respect is like air. If you take it away, it is all people think about.

- Watch for signs that show people are defending their dignity.
- Make it safe for everyone to add their information.
- All ideas must be safe to find their way out into the open.
- How do I express uncomfortable feedback?
- How do I speak persuasively — not abrasively?
- How do we get people to talk when they seem nervous?
- How do we move from thought to action?
- How do we add information and build on the relationship?

People feel safe receiving feedback because they trust the motives and abilities of the other person.

WARNING SIGNS
Silence —
Masking — not expressing true feelings.
Avoiding — steering away from a sensitive subject
Withdrawing — pulling out of the conversation altogether

BAD BEHAVIORS
Violence — any behavior that compels another toward your point of view
Controlling — coercing others to your way of thinking
Labeling — stereotyping people
Feeling of safety comes from mutual purpose and mutual respect.

Speak persuasively not abrasively — make it safe for others.

Confidence — Speak directly to the person you have the problem with.
Humility — Realize you don't have all the answers and ask for other's opinions.

Be sincere, curious and patient.

QUOTES

Find your passion and help others find theirs.

What you are thunders so loudly that I cannot hear what you say to the contrary.
— *Ralph Waldo Emerson*

We cannot exaggerate the significance of a strong determination to achieve a goal or realize a vision, a conviction, or even a passion.

The quiet sermon — If you don't stand for something, you'll fall for anything.
— *Alexander Hamilton*

"When you engage in a work professional, community, family that taps your talent and fuels your passion — that rises out of a great need in the world that you feel drawn by conscience to meet — therein lies your voice, your calling, your soul's code."

> — *The 8th Habit: From Effectiveness to Greatness*[4] by Stephen R. Covey

- Deep knowledge. Be aware of disturbances before disturbances happen.
- Be sensitive and responsive.
- Leaders try to consider potential problems and prevent them.
- Be aware of the ramifications of decisions.

People want to be part of an organization that is doing good and making a difference.

- Gems are found by sifting through tons of useless rock.
- When you acknowledge failure as a natural step in any growing process, you will develop and support the courage to take risks.
- Quantum leaps happen if you have a passion, a purpose and a plan.
- If you add persistence, your action will propel forward.
- One of the common denominators of most successful organizations is a commitment to other people — genuine caring for others and a contribution to their success.
- Consistent caring connections create commitment.

Commitment comes from the Latin —To ignite action and bring together those with the courage to commit — the ones with passion, energy and enthusiasm.
When you are committed to something you accept no excuses.

---

[4] Covey, Stephen R.. *The 8th habit*. (Egypt: Free Press, 2004), 85.

16. Influencer: The Power to Change Anything

By Kerry Patterson, Joseph Grenny, David Maxfield, Ron McMillan & Al Switzler

- Be aware of the threats.
- In order to improve our situation, what action must I take?
- The greatest persuader is a personal experience.
- Speak up early and honestly about problems.
- Make the "undiscussable" — discussable.
- It is the desire to be accepted, connected and respected that pulls the human heart strings.
- Be candid — take the risk to be honest.

Provide the exact steps a person must take to "Eat the Elephant." One step at a time.
Credit is definitely divisible — give it away any chance you get.

17. Monday Morning Choices: 12 Powerful Ways to Go from Everyday to Extraordinary

By David Cottrell

Put your goals into words and then get busy.
If you can dream it, you can do it.
Never lose sight of the fact that this whole thing (Disneyland) was started by a mouse.

Standing in the middle of the road is very dangerous; you get knocked down by the traffic from both sides.

—*Margaret Thatcher*

There is no pillow as soft as a clear conscience.

—John Wooden

If you think you're too small to have an impact, try going to bed with a mosquito in the room.

—Dame Anita Roddick

Having the world's best idea will do you no good unless you act on it.
People who want milk shouldn't sit on a stool in the middle of the field in hopes that a cow will back up to them.

—Curtis Grant

You can't build a reputation on what you are "going to do."

—Henry Ford

Even if you are on the right track, you'll get run over if you just sit there.

—Will Rogers

If you want to win, you must "stay in the game."
Don't let temporary failure cause you to miss out on permanent success.

You can't change the fruit unless you change the root.
Our root is our attitude.

18. Lincoln on Leadership: Executive Strategies for Tough Times

By Donald Phillips

"Get out of the office and circulate among the troops." — Get to know your people.

Build strong alliances — A house divided against itself cannot stand.

Attention — It's all there is and trust is learned by example.

Persuade rather than coerce — A drop of honey catches more flies than a gallon of gall. Elevate your people.

Character, honesty and integrity — Always do what you say you are going to do

Never act out of vengeance or spite — Kindness, empathy and positive end results are most important.

"Let us have faith that right makes might, and in that faith, let us, to the end, dare to do our duty as we understand it."

It often takes more courage to dare to do right than to fear to do wrong.

Set goals and be results oriented.

Find the people who make things happen.
Encourage innovation —The question is "Can we do better?"

Great leaders are not only instruments of change but catalysts of change.
Adopt a "more than one way to skin a cat" attitude.

Communication
Master the art of public speaking.
Lincoln communicated with simple and straight forward statements.

Lincoln built credibility by being consistent and clear when speaking to others.

He did it with more than words. His actions always mirrored what he said.
Communicate with stories. People are often influenced by broad humorous illustrations.

As a leader you need to communicate your vision — clearly and concisely.
Lincoln was always open to all impressions or influences of others.

He aimed for a new level of awareness by listening to his people.
He was open, civil, tolerant and fair and maintained respect for the dignity of people at all times.

19. How the Mighty Fall: And Why Some Companies Never Give In

By Jim Collins (Author of Good to Great: Why Some Companies Make the Leap... and Others Don't and Built to Last: Successful Habits of Visionary Companies)

It was thought that most companies "fall" because of complacency. They fail to stimulate innovation, fail to initiate bold action, fail to ignite change. They just become lazy and watch the world pass them by.

This answer, however, does not support the data.

Overreaching. Trying to do too much. Much better explains how the once invincible self-destruct.

If I were to pick one marker above all others to use as a warning sign, it would be a declining proportion of key seats filled with the right people.

- The most important thing is what does the member care about?
- A great company is a series of well-executed actions that add up on top of each other.
- Have calm deliberate action. Take one shot at a time.
- Organizations do not die from lack of earnings. They die from lack of cash.
- What do great companies have in common? All have taken a great fall and recovered. Truly successful companies have come back from a great setback.
- Success is falling down and getting up one more time.
- Nothing great happens without passion and the right people displaying remarkable intensity.
- The signature of mediocrity is constant inconsistency.
- Have a constant sense of urgency that never changes.

Stages of failure for companies

1. Hubris born of success. "We are so great we can do anything." Don't stray from the core that made your company successful in the first place. A CORE VALUE that meets a fundamental human need, SOMETHING YOU DO that you have become best in the world at. Take care of the organization and preserve its specific practices and methods.
2. Undisciplined pursuit of "more." Overreaching better captures how the mighty fall.
   Always looking for the "NEXT BIG THING" to do instead of working on making what you are doing NOW – EXCEPTIONAL.
3. Denial of risk and peril. Vigorous fact base data disappears.
4. Grasping for salvation. Get back to the discipline that brought greatness in the first place. Finding a "silver bullet" doesn't work.
5. Capitulation of irrelevance or death.

Organizational decline is largely self-inflicted.
How do you go from iconic to irrelevant?
Are there clearly stages of decline?

20. Think Big, Act Small: How America's Best Performing Companies Keep the Start-up Spirit Alive

By Jason Jennings

This book describes the secrets of the most profitable and fastest growing companies in the United States.

- It is not the big that eat the small — it's the fast and flexible that eat the slow.
- Be accessible, transparent, trustable, and frugal — praise others.
- Stay in the trenches.
- 96% of brand extensions fail.
- Nail the fundamentals.
- The most common thing about common sense is how uncommon it is.
- Solve customer's/member's problems — listen and act.
- Make something better that creates value.
- An organization won't have a long-term future, unless action on short-term objectives is achieved.
- Let go of what is no longer working.
- Get every member and staff to think and act like owners.
- Build communities of raving fans.
- The biggest thrill is to identify and help build future leaders.

Guiding Principles
Integrity, compliance, value creation, customer service, entrepreneurship, customer focus, knowledge, embrace change, stewardship.

Work ethic, stand for something, humility, respect, willing to "get your hands dirty."

- How do priorities get on the menu? The member decides.
- Remarkable companies are able to grow because they are not burdened by a five-year plan.
- Take care of your core business.
- When the bulk of your revenue is based on renewing the same members every year, genuine value is placed on the work you do and the long-term relationships you build.
- We must strive to exceed the member's expectations.
- Search for the "wow" to replace the "okay."

21. Race for Relevance

By Harrison Coerver and Mary Byers

When changes in the environment are significant'
Incremental adjustments are inadequate.

- Before today — Associations were slow and risk adverse
- Now — Members are demanding value
- Competitors are offering the same services, members have diverse and conflicting interests.
- Pressures of time and generational differences create a need for radical change.

Five radical changes

- Overhaul governance model and committee experience Empower CEO and staff expertise Rigorously define the member market
- Rationalize programs and services
- Build a robust technology frame work
** Organizations must have profit and direction.

They must align resources with results and the need to optimize resources.

- What am I getting for my dues dollar?
- Focus on how to help members be more successful!
- Deliver value that is both convenient and accessible

Marketplace realities that have changed the field

1. **Time** — Members are busy and pressed for time
   Information overload — Getting their attention is the problem
2. **Value** — In response to demand for ROI (Return on Investment) Increasing the "stuff" increasing the menu of programs and services — But unused services have no value
   - Programs about generating non-dues revenue — Money spent on this might have been better spent on creating and communicating value.
   - We must determine member needs, issues and problems and come up with solutions.
   - If members have to hunt through long lists to find value, most don't even try.
   Why? Because they are busy.
3. **Market Value** — Our membership is increasingly diverse.
   - It is difficult to be all things to all people.
   - If we don't distinguish ourselves from our competitors at least in some way, we will be invisible.
4. **Competition** — Associations compete for readership of publications and attendance at meetings.
   - People are not likely to renew if they do not perceive value and are in several organizations
   - We are also competing with online search
   - Convenience and cost are the reason people don't go to meetings.
   - Perhaps competing organizations could look to collaborate.

5. **Technology**
   - Online education is becoming the norm.

Overhaul the Governance model

Almost all boards are effectively governed by about five people.

Directors need the following skills:

1. Understanding Technology
2. Relationships and political savvy
3. Financially competent
4. Product development and marketing
5. Visionary
   - Boards should address gender, ethnicity, youth, size and geography.
   - Leaders should have the following core competencies: vision, resilience, flexibility, open-mindedness, passion, commitment.
6. Committees
   Most committees don't have a clear understanding of what they are supposed to do — staff does most of the work.
   - Empower the CEO and staff to lead committees — get the right people on the bus in the right seats.
   - What is the value of your organization to the member?

Suggested Radical Change
- Provide a consulting service.
- The more service, the more dues.

***Identify the association's unique abilities that can be matched with the emerging marketplace.

- Lay out a plan — set a direction then…
Communicate, Communicate, Communicate

- Rationalize programs, services and activities.
- What gets measured, gets improved.

If you try to chase two rabbits, you will lose them both.

— *Leonard Nimoy*

22. Profiles in Courage

By John F. Kennedy

People who recognize what needs to be done — do it.
None of us can stand to be lookers on or critics from the sidelines.
Show patience, restraint and compassion as well as wisdom, strength and courage.

Courage is grace under pressure.
I will speak in spite of the intimidators or threats.

23. The Elephant and The Ant

By Vince Poscente

The only thing that will redeem mankind is cooperation.
Dream the impossible.
For some the sky is the limit.
For him it was just the beginning.
Unite our land.

The ideal for any warrior is to lay down his sword.
Gratitude is the magic ingredient in the recipe for fulfilling life.
The definition of insanity is doing the same thing over and over and expecting different results.

The chain of negativity is a pattern.
No two thoughts can occupy the same place at the same time.
Visualizing 100% of the scenarios in which you handle tough situations will build a rock solid platform.

Without conflict or struggle there is no growth.

- The worthiest goals take time and energy.
- Scarcity mentality is lack of vision.
- Focus on having instead of wanting.
- Goals must be in alignment for something significant to occur.
- Never underestimate the power of emotions.
- By tapping into your emotions you will find out what motivates you.
- Your passions will ignite your vision.
- I feel connected, respected and alive.
- Make fear your friend not your master.
- As you live your life you realize the importance of living without regret over what might have been.

—Will you look back and wonder if you could have done more?
—Will you look back and question whether you gave it all you had?
—If you can look back and have no regrets, then you know you have done your best and your best can take you to places beyond your wildest expectations.

The power within aligned by the power of many is equivalent to a tiny ant guiding a mighty elephant.

—Vince Poscente

24. The 8th Habit: From Effectiveness to Greatness

By Stephen R. Covey

From effectiveness to greatness.
How to be a stronger more effective and truly inspiring leader.
A call to action for twenty-first century leaders.

A leader has:

1. A clear understanding of what the organization is trying to achieve.
2. Clear team and organizational goals.
3. High-trust environment.
4. Fosters open communication, respectful of differing opinion
5. May result in new and better ideas.
6. Holds people accountable.

There is an organizational cost of failing to freely engage passion, talent and intelligence of the workforce.

—Reaching beyond effectiveness.
—The call for a new era is greatness ... for fulfillment, passionate execution, and significant contribution.

—*The 8th Habit* asks us to find our voice and help others find theirs.
—We all have boundless potential to serve the common good.
—This voice encompasses the soul of the organizations that will survive, thrive and profoundly impact the future of the world.

Engage is a work that taps your talent, fuels your passion and rises out of a great need in the world that you feel drawn by conscience to meet — therein lies your voice.

"When you engage in a work that taps your talent and fuels your passion — that rises out of a great need in the world that you feel drawn by conscience to meet — therein lies your voice, your calling, your soul's code."[5]

—*Stephen R. Covey*

[5] Covey, *The 8th Habit*, 85.

—See a need and fill it!

—Vision comes as people sense human need and respond trying to meet that need.

Few of us can do great things, but all of us can do small things with great love.

—*Mother Teresa*

Four basic needs of human beings are to:

- Live
- Love
- Learn
- Leave a legacy

Live like you were dying!

At the personal level these organizations are filled with bright, talented people at every level who feel straight jacketed, undervalued, and uninspired. They are frustrated and don't feel that they have the power to change things.

- Most ailing organizations develop a functional blindness to their own defects — they can't see their problems.
- Deep within each of us is an inner longing to live a life of contribution.
- The Latin for inspire is "To breathe life into another."
- The best way to get people to learn is to turn them into teachers.

Awareness

The range of what we think and do is limited by what we fail to notice.

4 Intelligences: Mental, Physical, Emotional and Self-knowledge

- Awareness, social sensitivity, empathy, ability to communicate, courage to acknowledge weaknesses and express and respect differences.
- Intuition will tell the "thinking mind" where to look next.
- Research has shown that in the long run emotional intelligence is a better determinant for success.
- Relating well with others.

Emotional Intelligence 2.0 is a book with a test at the end that tells you how you do with emotional intelligence — well worth the price of the book.

—Spiritual intelligence is linked to humanity's need for meaning.

—Scientific evidence, largely from the field of neuroscience, finds that humans are wired to connect with others. Meeting the basic needs for connections is essential to health and human flourishing.

—The whole concept behind finding your voice and helping others find theirs is a synergistic concept.

—Profound influence comes from vision, discipline and passion.

Imagination is more important than knowledge.

—Albert Einstein

—Leadership is the capacity to translate vision into reality.

—That you may retain your self-respect, it is better to displease people by doing what you know is right.

—Great leaders seek out and value the opinions of others. They don't pretend they have all the answers.

—Greatness requires a passionate purpose and must be driven by core business practices that foster reward, collaboration, growth and commitment.

Find your voice and inspire others to find theirs.

"We can see far into the distance that anything is possible — small consistent changes can make huge results."
                    —*The Tipping Point: How Little Things Can Make*
                    a Big Difference[6] *by Malcom Gladwell*

Be willing to experience discomfort to reach your goal.

"When you engage in a work that taps your talent and fuels your passion — that rises out of a great need in the world that you feel drawn by conscience to meet — therein lies your voice, your calling, your soul's code."[7]

                                        —*Stephen R. Covey*

Clarity of vision — goal with deep meaning
Commitment — positive dominant thoughts
Consistency — baby steps, every day
Control — respond to unforeseen events

---

[6] Gladwell, Malcolm. The Tipping Point: How Little Things Can Make a Big Difference. (United States: Wheeler Pub., 2003).
[7] Covey, The 8th Habit, 85.

LIVE   LOVE   LEAVE A LEGACY

25. The Tipping Point: How Little Things Can Make a Big Difference

By Malcom Gladwell

Social Epidemics are driven by a handful of very exceptional people.

Connectors, Maven (Have the Information), Salesmen (Sell it) (Energy, enthusiasm, charm and likability)

When people are in a group and the responsibility for acting is diffused, they assume someone else will act.

Stickiness factor — Emphasis, excitement, volume

- Repeat six times
- Build a level of trust
- Emotional contagion — mimicry — you smile, I smile.
- Interactive learning through repetition.

Law of the few
- Stickiness factor of your message
- Power of content
- Vehicle of persuasion — one-on-one
- A small change in content or action can TIP an epidemic. (Washing hands can prevent an epidemic.)
- Peer and community influence are very strong.

26. Beyond Emotional Intelligence

By Jim Karol & Dale Ledbetter

Compassion is the keen awareness of the interdependence of things.

Three of the key elements in the "art of working together" are:

- How to deal with change
- How to deal with conflict
- How to reach our potential

People sometimes:

- Feel beaten up
- Feel nervous or manipulated
- Speak or act petty
- Don't feel heard, respected or acknowledged for the things that they do.

Often management ignores emotional realities and has little connection to what people are actually thinking and feeling.

Roles tell us who we are within a group.
What we can and cannot say and do and at times how we can interact.

Common invisible rules:

- Pretend you are happy with your job, even if you aren't.
- Make the boss look good even if they make you look bad.
- Act like you know what you are doing, even if you don't.
- Protect management from anything negative no matter what.

Loyalty is the most important thing — don't question the companies methods.

If you are unhappy with these "invisible rules," then leave. Don't try to change things.

These invisible rules are often at odds.

- Change creates imbalance. People feel threatened and defensive patterns emerge.
- Change is a test of organizations as well as individuals.
- Each must maintain a delicate balance between being stable and being flexible.
- When there is a lot of change proposed, individuals and organizations tend to tighten up and become ridged in order to deal with chaos and confusion.

Management can send out mixed messages and doesn't take a stand on issues.

The company may be managed by crisis and always be in a state of emergency.

Staffs are not kept informed of changes or problems.

Management looks for "quick fixes" rather than long-term solutions.

You can't talk about feelings or conflicts — or better ways of doing things even though changes could make you more productive.

As with *The Emperor's New Clothes* by Hans Christian Andersen, "Many leaders have people who tell them what they think they want to hear, instead of what they need to hear."

- Create an environment where honest well-intended feedback is encouraged, honored and cherished and complete truth is valued.

- Change the behaviors that do not serve others.
- A powerful vision lifts people up and unites them.
- Do good in the world.

SMART — Specific, Measurable, Motivating, Attainable, Relevant and Tractable.

Don't be so future oriented that you drive the present out of your life.

The way you listen speaks volumes.

If we wait for the perfect answer, the world will pass us by.

— Jack Welch

How often as a leader, how many times a day, a week,
a month, do we pass up the opportunity to thank those
people in our lives, or businesses and our organizations
who are "doing the heavy lifting to help us be successful,"
who are in the shadows doing the work, who are
"packing our parachutes" so we have a safe landing?

"The greatest management principle in the world is: 'The things that get rewarded and appreciated get done."

—The Greatest Management Principle
in the World[8] by Michael LeBoeuf

[8] LeBoeuf, Michael. The Greatest Management Principle in the World. (United States: Berkley Books, 1989).

27. Quantum Leap Thinking

By James J. Mapes

1. Pay attention
2. Turn fear into power
3. Hold a vision
4. Enlarge goals
5. Be flexible
6. Have commitment
7. Empower
8. Communicate with integrity
9. Create partnership
10. Have fun
11. Take risks
12. Trust
13. Love
14. Support

Creative Thinking   Continuous Learning   Managing Change

The Successful Attitude

Grit — The power to persevere.
Success demands a fierce inner fire and a drive to persist against all obstacles.

Winners — They love to go head-to-head with other people.
It is critically important to keep going after failure.

High achievers —
- Stick it out
- Are constantly driven to improve
- Never satisfied
- Persevere

- Ferocious determination and direction
- Resilient and hard working
- Passion plus persistence = GRIT

Grittier kids went further and worked more hours.
Our potential is one thing. What we do with that potential is quite another.
"Get up one more time!"

Mindset —You will succeed.
Help people be great competitors — perseverance.

I love the poem "The Race" by D. H. "Dee" Groberg
The message: "Get up each time you fall."

- Social Support was a far greater predictor of happiness than any other factor.
- Happiness leads to success when you feel socially connected and supported and the person feels their work is important.
- They view stress as a challenge.

Happiness + Optimism and Social Connections = Enhanced performance.

We live in a world dominated by collaboration. So, the ability to make the group more than the sum of its parts to establish a meaningful connection with another person matters more and more.

Modeling giving behavior

- Praising children when they are seen giving a helping hand or caring for a friend.
- Prepare children to face struggle and overcome it.
- Praise children for effort, strategy and resilience.

- Children should be open to new experiences.
- Achieving at a high level takes work and diligence.
- Learn to be kind to oneself when things don't work out.
- All successful people struggle through setbacks.
- Reduce the fear of failure.
- Control what we pay attention to.
- Mindfulness training is vital.

Achievement takes preparation.
Upbringing, education and life experiences play a more significant role than genetics in determining success.

The key factor in the level of achievement is not innate or genetic but the deliberate practice of a skill.

The attitude is important – the growth mindset = **HARD WORK**

Vincent van Gogh, a Dutch Impressionist, became famous after his death. He sold one painting in his lifetime and shot himself at age 37.
In a decade he created 2,100 works of art including 860 oil paintings (most in his last two years.)

Great things are done by a series of small things brought together.
—Vincent van Gogh

Love many things, for therein lies the true strength, and whosoever loves much — performs much, and can accomplish much, and what is done in love is done well.
—Vincent van Gogh

Non-cognitive ability is more closely tied to success more than IQ, cooperation, self-control, growth, mindset, and social competence.
—Leslie Gutman and Ingrid Schoon

I've learned that people will forget what you said, people will forget what you did, but people will never forget how you made them feel.

—*Maya Angelou*

Don't let the "noise of other's opinions" drown out your inner voice.
— *Steve Jobs, Stanford University commencement speech, 2005*

Sometimes life hits you in the head with a brick.
Do what you love!
Your time is limited.
Don't waste it living someone else's life.
If you live each day as if it were your last, someday you will be right.
Express what makes your heart sing.
Effective leaders move others to action.

— *Steve Jobs*

Steve Jobs never graduated from college. In fact, he did not go to college and was adopted.

28. Leading Change

By John P. Kotter

Two people who will kill teamwork — those with egos and those who are snakes and create mistrust.

- A sense of urgency is needed for change.
- Lack of communication — Activities need to create mutual understanding, respect and caring associated with trust.
- A common goal allows teamwork to happen.
- Vision with urgency is a central component of leadership.
- Clarify the direction.
- Facilitating change that is not necessarily in a person's short-term best interest may be needed.

6. Characteristics of effective visions

Imaginable - Conveys a picture of the future
Desirable - Appeals to members
Feasible - Realistic attainable goal
Focused - Clear enough to provide guidance in decision-making
Flexible - Allows individual initiative
Communicable - Can explain vision in five minutes.

The vision must appeal to most people who have a stake
in the organization.

Strategy - How the vision will be accomplished — what will
be done; it has to be measurable.

Lip service without commitment creates a dangerous illusion.

SIMPLE CLEAR COMMUNICATION
Multiple forms, repetition
Leadership by example, two-way communication

REPEAT/REPEAT/REPEAT - Find ways to tie the conversation.
Back to the big picture — Need to engage member's hearts and minds.

Lifelong learners take risks and careful listening and honest feedback is important.

EMPOWERMENT - Helps people give their opinion and be part of the action.

MAJOR INTERNAL TRANSFORMATION - Rarely happens unless many people assist. Structural barriers need to be removed to make this happen.
SHORT-TERM WINS ARE VERY IMPORTANT - Whenever you "let up" before the job is done is critical because momentum can be lost and regression may follow.

VERY HARD WORK CAN BE UNDONE QUICKLY - The organization of the future and the globalization of economy requires a high-urgency rate. Look for problems and opportunities to do it now and make things more efficient.

CANDID DISCUSSIONS - Must be valued and honest.

CANDID Cultures - Must be created.

Valid Data from a number of sources - A broad communication in the organization and willingness to deal honestly with feedback will go a long way toward squashing complacency and a sense of urgency to deal with a rapidly changing environment.

**Management deals with today.
Leadership deals with change
Successful organizations need to become
incubators for change.**

---

29. Inside the Nonprofit Boardroom

By Charles William Golding & Craig W. Stewart

What is a board? A group of people charged with the health, preservation and progress of an organization.

What is a trustee? People with the responsibility to nurture, care and protect the entire organization.

Qualities of a Trustee

1. **Integrity** - Keep the organization on the straight and narrow Do what you say you are going to do
2. **Judgement** - Help the board choose the right course and project
3. the future ramifications of decisions
4. **Perspective** - Keep a balance
5. **Courage** - Hold firm in your belief
6. **Creativity** - Come up with new ideas
7. **Dependability** - Attend all meetings and calls
8. **Stability** - Be prepared
9. **Sensitivity** - Be aware of individual needs. Address all issues even if they are presented by a minority.

The passionate trustee needs to "burn with desire for the cause."

- They hold the organization in the palm of their hand and protect it.
- They ask questions and thank the staff.
- They observe how their constituents are doing.

COMMUNICATION - Board of trustees rarely communicate with the people they represent. This is a mistake. Never forget "thank-yous" and give credit to the people who are working at the grassroots level.

30. The 21 Irrefutable Laws of Leadership: Follow Them and People will Follow You

By John C. Maxwell

These laws can be learned or can stand alone and are the foundation of leadership.
A leader must do many things well, but no one does all 21 things well — that is the importance of the team.

The greater number of laws you learn, the greater leader you will be.

Why is Warren Buffet such a great leader?
He is able to take a very complex situation, simplify it and teach it to others.
People listen because he has led a lifetime of success stories.

The Law of the Lid

- Whatever you want to accomplish is restricted by your ability to lead others.
- The greater the impact you want to make, the greater your influence needs to be.
- To reach your highest level of effectiveness, you need to rip off the lid.
- To change the direction of the organization, you need to change the leader

The Law of Influence

Mother Teresa - The quintessential, energetic entrepreneur, who had a perceived need and did something about it.

She built an organization against all odds, formulated its constitution and sent out branches all over the world. When she spoke people listened because her motives are pure and she tells the truth.

- Titles don't matter when it comes to leadership
- Leadership must be earned
- When a leader speaks, people listen because they are trusted
- People trust a track record.

The Law of Process

- Do it one day at a time — consistency
- Spend your whole life building
- Never stop learning
- To a person of action nothing is an obstacle
- Leadership requires perseverance
- Leadership is developed in a lifetime.

A Good leader remains focused.

—Jack Welch

They see the whole trip in their minds before they leave the dock.

—John C. Maxwell

The Law of Navigation

- Anyone can steer the ship but it takes a leader to chart the course.
- For a leader to be a good navigator they must reflect on things that have failed and learn from past experiences.
- Preparation, forethought and attention to detail are vital for a leader.
- A leader is one who sees more than others see, who sees farther than others see and who sees before others see.
- First rate navigators always have in mind that people are depending on them.

- Good navigators examine the facts before committing.
- Good navigators listen to what others have to say.
- Good navigators get their ideas from many sources.
  They talk to people in their organizations to find out what is happening at the grassroots level.
- They spend time with people outside their organization who can mentor them.
- They always rely on a team, not just on themselves.
- Must have a positive attitude but also be able to face facts realistically.
- Realistic leaders are objective enough to minimize illusions. They understand that self-deception can cost them their vision.
- Always have an analysis and daily review of your plan.

From the book titled *Good to Great: Why Some Companies Make the Leap... and Others Don't*[9] by Jim Collins, "You must retain faith that you will prevail. In the end you must confront the most brutal facts of your current reality."

The Law of Addition

- Leaders add value by serving others.
- James Sinegal (Owner and founder of Costco along with Jeffrey Brotman) says:
  "To be successful, pay your people well and give them credit.
  If you can't give credit, you'll take the blame and you will drown in your inability to inspire."
- There is one critical question, "Are you making things better for the people who follow you?"
- True leaders are less interested in their position and more interested in their positive impact on others.

---

[9] Collins, Jim., Collins, James Charles. Good to Great: Why Some Companies Make the Leap...and Others Don't. (United Kingdom: HarperCollins, 2001).

Have an attitude of service

- We add value to others when we truly value them.
- When a person moves into a position of authority he or she gives up the right to abuse others.
- A servant leader must be open, trusting and caring offering their help and willing to be vulnerable.
- We must know and relate to what others value. We do this by listening.
- Inexperienced leaders are quick to lead before they know anything about those that they are leading.
- Respect others.
- Perform small acts of service for others without recognition or credit for themselves.

The Law of Solid Ground

- Trust is the most important thing for a leader.
- It is the glue that holds the organization together.
- A leader builds trust by constantly and consistently exemplifying competence, connection and character.
- If you make a commitment, keep it.
- Honesty, discipline and hard work exhibit character.

The Law of Respect

- People naturally follow leaders stronger than themselves.
- Respect for others is vital.
- Courage, a leader does not deserve the name unless they occasionally stand alone.
- Good leaders do what is right even at the risk of failure, in the face of great danger and under the brunt of relentless criticism.
- Success, loyalty and adding value to others is all necessary.

The Law of Intuition

- Decisions depend on so much more than just facts.
- Leaders use intuition to "read" a room, read future trends and sense when a group is frustrated or excited.
- Who you are and your past experiences dictate what you "see."
- Sometimes this dictates a new CEO and a new direction.

The Law of Magnetism

- Who you are determines whom you attract.
- Positive people attract others.
- The organization usually takes on the attitudes of its top leaders.

The Law of Connection

- Great leaders stand in front of a platoon and see 44 individuals, each of whom has aspirations, wants to live and do good.
- To connect with people in a group, relate to them as individuals.
- Leaders touch a heart before they ask for a hand.
- You can't move people to action unless you first connect with them through emotion.
- Be confident and be yourself.
- Be open and sincere.
- Focus on others — not yourself.
- Connect with people because you think they have value.
- It is the leader's job to initiate the connection.
- People don't care how much you know until they they know how much you care.
- Make yourself available, listen and give appreciation.
- The most important is to listen.
- Build relationship bridges.

The Law of the Inner Circle

- A leader's potential is determined by those closest to them.
- Nobody does anything great alone.
- Leaders have to deliver. There is no substitute
- for performance, but they need help to do this.
- The leader finds greatness in the group and he or she helps members find greatness in themselves.
- The leader must have the ability to influence those who influence others.
- There are people who lift and people who lean.

The Law of Empowerment

- Only secure leaders give power to others.
- The best executives pick good people to do the work and have the sense to stop meddling while they are doing it.
- To lead well we must help others reach their potential.
- A good leader gives some of their power away so that others may grow.
- The second barrier to empowerment is the resistance to change.
- The third barrier is the lack of self-worth, worrying how you look and what others may think —worrying whether you will be liked.
- To those who have confidence in themselves, change is simultaneous because they believe one person can make a difference and influence what goes on around them.

The greatest things happen only if you give others the credit.

- Leadership must be based on goodwill.
- Leadership means obvious and wholehearted commitment to helping followers.

Good leaders bring strength through diversity and mutual challenge.

- If you push people down, you will go down with them.
- Leaders must encourage change and continually improve their organizations.

The Law of the Picture

- People do what people see.
- Lead by example — take risks you ask your members to take.
- Be in front leading the charge and don't be afraid to get your hands dirty.
- Mission provides purpose answering, "Why?"
- Vision provides a picture answering, "What?"
- Strategy provides a plan answering, "How?"
- Nothing is more confusing than people who give good advice but set a bad example.

Leaders tell but never teach until they practice what they preach.

Poll asking what workers valued most in leaders:

- Leading by example, 26%
- Strong ethics or morals, 19%
- Knowledge of the business, 17%
- Fairness,14%
- Intelligence and competence, 10%
- Recognition of the employee,10%

The Law of Buy-in

- People don't follow worthy causes at first.
- They follow worthy leaders who promote causes they believe in.

The Law of Victory

- Victorious leaders find a way to win.
- They are unwilling to accept defeat.
- When the pressure is on, great leaders are at their best.
- Whatever is inside them comes to the surface.
- A team wins if they have unity of vision and passion to match.

The Law of the Big Mo

- You cannot kindle a fire in anyone's heart until it is burning in your own.
- Display enthusiasm at all times.
- Motivation is the key to developing momentum.
- Help your people and celebrate their accomplishments.

The Law of Priorities

- A leader is the one who climbs the tallest tree, surveys the entire situation and yells, "wrong jungle."
- Sometimes leaders need to think outside the box, reinvent the box and sometimes blow up the box.
  When you are the leader, everything is on the table.

Every year it is important to reprioritize the top 20% of activities that will have 80% of the returns.

- Activity is not always accomplishment.
- What is required to be exceptional?
- What brings the most success to our members?
- What brings the greatest reward?

The Law of Sacrifice

- Sacrifice is at the heart of leadership.
- There is no success without sacrifice.
- The heart of leadership is putting others ahead of yourself.

The Law of Timing

- The wrong action at the wrong time can lead to disaster.
- Leaders must have a full grasp on the situation and have confidence and decisiveness.
- Leaders must have experience and intuition and be incredibly organized and prepared.
- The right action at the right time will bring success.

The Law of Explosive Growth

- To add growth, lead followers.
- To multiply growth, lead leaders.
- Leaders are naturally impatient.
- If you develop leaders, your organization will experience explosive growth.
- If leaders develop the best, the best will help the rest.
- Leaders who develop leaders focus on strengths, treat individuals different, invest time in others, grow by multiplication, and impact people beyond their reach.
- What prompts attendees to become leaders is the influence of another leader 85% of the time.
- If you keep adding value to the leaders you lead, then they will be willing to stay with you.

The Law of Legacy

- A leader's lasting value is measured by succession.
- Great leaders pass the baton.
- A legacy is created only when a person puts their organization into the position to do great things without them.
- We have made a start in discovering the meaning of human life when we plant shade trees under which we know we will never sit.
- A life is not significant except for the impact on other lives.

31. 7 Measures of Success: What Remarkable Associations Do That Others Don't

By American Society of Association Executives (ASAE)

What Remarkable Associations Do That Others Don't

- Board size is not significant.
- Candidates for boards should be selected based on their skill, knowledge and experience.

CEOs of outstanding organizations successfully match themselves to the personality of the organization.

- Most organizations have a reserve fund of greater than 50% of expenses.
- The collaboration of staff is needed to answer the following questions:
- How can we serve the member? What do they need?
  Analyze current data and service the member.
- Remarkable organizations never forget their mission or their members, why they were we formed and whom they serve?
- Develop Big Harry Audacious Goals, BHAG.
- The culture is "family like" with a strong member focus.
- Be an action-organization with constantly exhibiting organization adaptability and alliance building.
- A lot of what we do is growth through selective mutation.
- Reinvent to adapt to new changes.
- The organization values its history but understands that what worked yesterday may not work today.
- Maintain a core purpose and willingly adapt how they do business to remain consistent with that purpose.
- Great organizations are often lead by shy, self-effacing and reserved people, more like Lincoln and Socrates.

- Have clearly stated goals and a disciplined process to achieve these goals.
- Remarkable leaders gather information from a variety of sources before making decisions. They create visionary thinking and create a culture of possibilities.
- Get the right people on the bus and the wrong people off.
- Develop a stop doing list to stop engaging in unproductive or inefficient activities.
- A "learning organization" transforms experience into knowledge.
- Is accessible to the whole organization and relevant to its core members. (5th Discipline)
- Is in a constant quest for improvement.
- Never stops improving the value they provide.
- All organizations must deal with setbacks and failures — but not all learn from them.
- Purposeful abandonment —We must prune to grow. Eliminate processes or programs that don't work.
- Great organizations are willing to admit what they can't do on their own.

SUMMARY:

- Commitment to purpose. We are here to serve you!
- Alignment of products or services.
- Commitment to analysis and feedback.
- CEO is a visionary and facilitates visionary thinking throughout the organization.
- Commitment to action. Respond to change
- Alliance building. Seek out partners and projects that complement their mission and purpose.
- Maintain a reserves greater than 50%.

32. Getting to Yes: Negotiating Agreement Without Giving In

By Roger Fisher, William L.Ury & Bruce Patton

Power of personal connection

- Meet face-to-face to humanize each of the parties.
- Don't have a desk or pedestal between you.
- Work through your problems face-to-face.
- Ask for advice and share your mistakes.
- If it is a joint meeting, sit side-by-side.
- Too often we fail to include those people who will be most impacted in the decision-making.

By excluding others we are impinging on their autonomy and will have to deal with their resentment from unilateral decisions.

However, if you ACBD (Always Consult Before Deciding), it can mean you will NGAD (Never Getting Anything Done).

- If you disagree, find merit.
- Unite in your reasoning and perspective.
- State back your understanding of their position.
- Listening needs to be active.
- Appreciate the other person.
- If it feels as though we are dancing to different music, ask how can we make this work for both sides?
- Ask others to hear what you are saying.
- Appreciation is a core concern.
- Everyone has a desire and deserves to feel understood.

33. Anyway: The Paradoxical Commandments Finding Personal meaning in a Crazy World

By Kent M. Keith & Spencer Johnson

Honesty and frankness make you vulnerable.
Be honest and frank anyway.

People are illogical, unreasonable and self-centered.
Love them anyway

If you do good, people will accuse you of selfish — ulterior motives.
Do good anyway

The good you do today will be forgotten tomorrow.
Do good anyway

The biggest men and women with the brightest ideas
can be shot down by the smallest men and women
with the smallest minds.
Think big anyway

34. The Art of Public Speaking

By Dale Carnegie

Nothing great was ever achieved without enthusiasm.
                                        — *Ralph Waldo Emerson*

- Express your authentic self — don't try to be something you are not.
- Want to help someone? Then shut-up and listen.

- The solution to winning more people to your argument is to tell more stories.
- Walk move and work the room.
- Use gestures sparingly.
- Passion, practice, presence.
- Deliver your talk in a genuine conversational way.
- How you say something leaves as deep an impression as what you say.
- 93% of a person's message is conveyed non-verbally.
- Believe in what you are saying.

Ditch the PowerPoint and speak from your heart

- Is what you are providing different and remarkable?
- Replace words with images.
- The brain cannot read PowerPoint slides and listen to you at the same time.
- If you add a picture, the recall rate increases by 65%.
- Pictures are stamped in our brain and more easily recalled.

Simplicity is the ultimate sophistication.

—Leonardo da Vinci

Our life is frittered away by detail… Simplicity, simplicity, simplicity.

—Henry David Thoreau

- Believe in something bigger than yourself.
- Force a hand and it will fight you, but convince a mind to think as you want it to by listening first and you have an ally.
- Before you can inspire them with any emotion you must believe yourself first.

Exceptional presenters radiate passion, conviction and enthusiasm.

- When presenting square up to the people you are talking to
- Stand tall, keep head and eyes up and connect with the audience
- Smile sincerely
- Lean into the person you are speaking to
- Move with purpose, energy and enthusiasm
- Nuts and bolts to presentations
- 60 second opening — short, focused and relevant
- Begin with a purpose
- Tell people what they are about to hear — frame your message
- Our current position — the next step
- Three things I would like you to think of today are...
- The key point I want you to remember is...
- If you remember one thing from my speech, remember this...
- My biggest concern is that we are relevant to our members
- By listening to their needs we help them...
- End with a purpose statement
- Use an attention-grabbing opener
- What is the greatest challenge facing our organization today?
- End with a sincere thank you — a quote.

Voice: Strong, positive

- Use your diaphragm and lungs and a range of inflection.
- Speak/pause/breathe — take your time — articulate your thoughts.
- Be deliberate — eliminate verbal graffiti (Examples: um, okay, "like," to be honest with you)

To earn their respect, you must first connect: Genuine interest in your message

- If you want to alienate your audience, first talk about yourself, read your speech use inappropriate humor

- Speak to the interests of your audience. What can I do for you?
- Be conversational, not stiff. Practice
- Short/focused/relevant. Use material that is based on "real-life" events
- Don't tell them what you have done
- Tell them what you are going to do for them
- The key point is...
- My objective is... The end result... next step.

The destiny of this organization is not a matter of chance. It is a matter of choice and deliberate action by each one of us to make things happen.

- Purpose, prepared, persistent
- Exceptional presenters radiate passion
- To persuade the audience — take action
- Nothing great can ever be achieved without enthusiasm
- See energy being transferred to others — enthusiasm for the event
- Leaning forward adds energy to your presentation
- Passion, excitement, enthusiasm, confidence and commitment
- An audience attention span is 15-30 seconds — continually regain the audience's attention
- Use visuals
- Use humor: I will not make age an issue of this campaign. I am not going to exploit for political purposes my opponent's youth and inexperience.

— Ronald Reagan.

Using a quote "off the cuff" demonstrates quick wit
The quickest way to connect to an audience is by demonstrating you understand their business issues.

Practice, Practice

We are what we repeatedly do. Excellence, then is not an act, but a habit.

— Will Durant

- Silence is golden when you can't think of a good answer.
- In order to be listened to, we must first listen and then ask to tell our side of the story.
- No dialog can occur if you take a shotgun and blow a hole in the face of your opponent.
- Open dialog and discourse is vital.

Even a mistake may turn out to be the one thing necessary for a worthwhile achievement.

—Henry Ford

How do you create a level of conviction? Passion — then tell your audience exactly what you want them to do.

Dream A belief that you can lead them to the impossible.

A successful team picks up on the leader's passion and share's the desire to win.

I dream things that never were and say, why not.

— Robert Francis "Bobby" Kennedy

It is consistent, progressive development that helps create world class results.

Believe - Legacies are created by those little daily consistencies of winning that add up to something that is enormous.

Risk -You have to be in it to win it.

You will miss every shot you do not take.

Sometimes you have to go way out on a limb to get the best fruit.

Measure - You can't improve unless you know the score.

Persevere - Even breakthrough teams experience conflict and failure. Don't focus on mistakes.

Tell stories - Breakthrough teams tell stories with passion.

Happiness - When what you think and what you do are in harmony. To connect with your audience your message must be honest and caring.
Don't badmouth the opposition — ever.

I DO is stronger than I don't.

- Speak simply with brief, clear, concise and easy to understand phrases.
- You need to be memorable.
- Nothing works as well as relevant stories told well.
- Begin with an anecdote.
- Offer a prediction, offer a dramatic forecast.
- Hook your audience into the first paragraph with a strong opening. *
- Tell the audience about things you are proud to have been a part of.
- Be the spark that ignites ideas.
- If attacked, don't take it personally.
- Win the game — don't deny — but inform and educate.
- Tell a story that contradicts the attack.

Qualities of a leader:

- Likeability
- Trustworthy
- Competent
- Experienced

- Part of a team
- Able and eager to participate
- Ready to listen
- Adaptable to change
- Eager to share credit
- A pause can be a powerful thing.
- All that matters is what the audience wants.
- Inform, persuade, inspire
- What makes a great speaker is having a conversation — sharing a small bit of information you think might improve their lives.
- Be informative, persuasive, inspiring and instructive.
- What is your audience looking for?
- People react to speakers who are warm, friendly, interesting, organized, confident, knowledgeable, creative and inspiring.
- Anticipate the question your audience brings to the presenter.

Listening matters - It is the central skill used in establishing relationships.

Active listening — demonstrates acceptance, promotes problem solving activities, shows you are receptive to others' ideas, and increases the self-esteem of the other person.

- Make sure your audience feels as smart as you are.
- Honesty is the most important. Don't put yourself up on a pedestal.
- Keep the speech simple, one to two main ideas they can use.
- Use a quotation to stimulate audience thinking.
- Focus on action — success lies in the details.
- The first rule for teaching other leaders is to "know your students."
- The second rule is "don't ever treat them like students."
- Leaders and members will "buy in" to your vision only if they have a part in developing it.
- Lead from the bottom up.

BE A SERVANT LEADER

- Leadership is action not position.
- Seek ways to build bridges.
- Leadership is not a matter of position, but of relationships.
- One-on-one personal encounters are necessary.
- If you lead other leaders, you must connect with them personally and take into account their interests.

35. Selling 101: What Every Successful Sales Professional Needs to Know

By Zig Ziglar

What every successful professional needs to know
- You don't persuade by telling — you persuade by asking.
- Emphasis on listening for the answers — great relationship builder.
- When asked a question respond with a question.
- Integrity means you do the right thing.
- With integrity you have nothing to fear because you have nothing to hide.
- Efficiency means doing things right.
- Effectiveness means doing the right things.
- Listen to needs and desires
- Talking is sharing.
- Listening is caring.
- Have a genuine interest and concern for other people.

Organization   Discipline   Commitment

Four Steps

1. **Needs Analysis** - The customer buys because they need or want something.
2. **Need Awareness** - Be sure you know what the need is by asking questions. We buy what the organization does for us.
3. **Need Solution** - Tell the person what the organization can do for them.
4. **Need Satisfaction** - Truly have a desire to help others and the person to benefit.
   Always ask for the "order."
   - When you ask "what do you think" questions, you establish trust.
   - Motivate the person to share needs, wants, problems and interests.
   - Ask questions to discover how the "customer" or member feels.
   - Most of us make emotional decisions.
   - Fear of loss is greater.

Can you see where joining this organization would be beneficial to you?

- Are you interested in growing?
- When do you think...?
- What do you mean by...?
- Tell me more about that...

Be a caring counselor — not an attorney. Interview.
We rarely take action until we are out of balance.

Why do your prospects "buy"?
People purchase tools that give them power over their past progress in the present and hope for the future.

We must clearly spell out the benefits "one-on-one":

- If you call, ask "Did I take you away from something important?"
- "May I ask you a couple of questions?"
- When you persist pleasantly and professionally, you will create a "win-win" solution.
- NO — means the person doesn't know enough.
- New decisions may be based on new information.
- From "no" to "know."
- Identify the objection… Empathize… Find out true objections

How does what you have to offer benefit the person?

KISS — KEEP IT SIMPLE — RECAP — THEN ASK

---

36. Raving Fans: Revolutionary Approach to Customer Service

By Ken Blanchard & Sheldon Bowles

The worst thing you can do is meet expectations sometimes, fall short other times, and exceed every now and then.

FLEXIBILITY

The perfect vision is constantly changing because the wants and the needs of the member are changing all the time.

- Flexibility and consistency. We must listen to the member and respect their input.

- Listening to the member is powerful. Responding to what they ask for is dynamite!
- If you are not riding the wave of change, you may find yourself beneath it.
- You need to be focused beyond your vision.
- Only an "up-to-the-minute vision" can create *Raving Fans.*
- The perfect vision is constantly changing because the wants and the needs of the members are constantly changing.

FLEXIBILITY IS VITAL

- The rule of 1% move ahead.
- What is delivered / How it's delivered.
- We must listen to the members and be flexible enough to meet their needs now.
- Alter your direction when they alter theirs.
- Listen to the member.
- Responding to what the customer says is dynamic.
- Take the vision and turn it into an action plan.
- Consistency/Ongoing improvement/Ability to alter the course quickly.
- Ask, listen and respect the members.
- Continually improve by 1%.

There are four things we cannot recover:

- The stone after the throw
- The word after it is said
- The occasion after the loss
- The time after it is gone.

Dare to soar - Your attitude determines your altitude in life.
Collaboration - Be the light that others can come to with their ideas, visions and dreams.

Never doubt that blending your talents with those of others can change the world.

Well done is better than well said.

— *Benjamin Franklin*

Together anything is possible.
A pessimist sees the difficulty in every opportunity.
The optimist sees the opportunity in every difficulty.

— *Winston Churchill*

When you reach the "end of your rope" tie a knot and hang on.

— *Franklin D. Roosevelt*

If you can't feed 100 people, then just feed one.
We shall never know the good that a simple smile can do..

—*Mother Teresa*

"Be the change you want to see in the world." Just do it!

— *Mahatma Gandhi*

**If you firehose information,
often all is lost.
Find your message. Keep it simple.
Repeat it often.**

Chapter 4

Poems

1. "The Bridge Builder"

A poem by Will Allen Dromgoole

An old man going down a lone highway
came in the evening cold and gray
to a chasm vast and deep and wide
through which was flowing a sullen tide
The old man crossed in the twilight dim;

That swollen stream held no fears for him;
But he turned when safe on the other side
and built a bridge to span the tide.

"Old Man" said a fellow pilgrim near;
You are wasting your strength with building here;
Your journey will end with the ending day;
You never again must pass this way;
You have crossed the chasm deep and wide
Why build you a bridge at the eventide?"

The builder lifted his old gray head.
"Good friend in the path I have come," he said.
"There followed after me today
a youth whose feet must pass this way.

143

This swollen stream that was naught to me
to that fair-haired youth may a pitfall be;
He too must cross in the twilight dim;
Good fiend, I am building this bridge for him.

BE a MENTOR — GET a MENTOR

2. PERSEVERE BOLDLY

The difference between perseverance and obstinacy is that one comes from a strong **will** and the other comes from a strong **won't**.
— *Henry Ward Beecher*

Know when to persist, but also know if you find yourself on a dead horse you may want to get off. If you find yourself in a hole you need to stop digging.

Prune to grow clean your closets
The best organizations know what to stop doing.

3. AUTHENTICITY

Integrity does not blow with the wind or change with the tide. It is the inner image of our true selves. Always be who you are because you are valued for your own special talents and ideas.

An authentic person is not affected by politics. They do what they feel is right — always!
— *John D. MacDonald*

Wisdom is knowing the right path to take and integrity is taking it.
— *W.H. McKee*

FEELINGS

You may never care what a person says or what a person knows but you will remember how they made you feel. This is the power of recognition and praise.

Caring Connections Create Commitment

This was the title of one of my first talks to an organization about membership.

If you notice each word starts with a C and so we have C-4, which is an explosive!

Caring is your lightening rod in most relationships.

4. PERSEVERANCE & PASSION

Go over, go under, go through but never give up. Get up each time you fall

Refuse to lose.

A leader's job is to look into the future and see the organization, not as it is, but as it should be.

— *Jack Welch*

Level 5 leaders have deep personal humility with an intense professional will.

They are honest, seeking mutual benefit. They are capable and can deliver!

They shine the light on others.

Two Key Skills — Listening & Speaking

Listening makes you captivating. We value that people care enough to listen.

Listen actively. Pause for a full second before responding.

People's heads go nowhere until their hearts lead them there.

- A great presentation inspires and moves people. Don't impress them.
- Move them!
- Beware of jokes when presenting.
- The only joke that works is when you poke fun at yourself.

5. COMMITMENT

Is what transforms a promise into reality.
It is the words that speak boldly of your intentions.
It is the actions that speak louder than words.
It is making the time when there is none
It is coming through time after time, year after year.
Commitment is the stuff character is made of — the power to change the face of things.

It is the daily triumph of integrity over skepticism.

— Abraham Lincoln

A Story About Van Cliburn

One evening after another magnificent concert, world renowned Pianist Harvey Lavan "Van" Cliburn Jr. was approached by an admirer who had been in the audience. The emotional fan grasped Cliburn's hand and said,

"I would give my life to be able to play like that."
Cliburn smiled and said, "I did."

Talent is overrated! People are successful because they have taken the responsibility to put in the work.

6. COURAGE & CONFIDENCE

A true leader has the confidence to stand alone, the courage to make tough decisions and the
compassion to listen to and act on the needs of others.
They are much like eagles. They don't flock — you find them one at a time.

The three most important traits a leader can have are: courage, patience and wisdom.

Two of the greatest qualities of Life are: Patience...

...and Wisdom

Courage and Confidence

There's no thrill in easy sailing when the skies are clear and blue.
There's no joy in merely doing things that anyone can do.
But there is some satisfaction that is mighty sweet to take,
When you reach a destination that you thought you'd never make.

—Spirella

7. REMEMBER & RECONNECT

Did you have a favorite teacher or someone who made a difference in your life?

Reconnect with them. Send them a note. Chances are very few people have ever let them know of the effect they had on their lives.

Put a note in your kid's lunches, or send them a letter in the mail. Tell them you love them every time you talk to them. None of us know when we will have another day together.

Seize the day!

The most attractive people in the world are the ones who are interested in others turned outward in cheerfulness, kindness and appreciation,
instead of turned inward to be constantly centered in themselves.

8. Which attitude will win? The one you feed

By Aïda Muluneh

"What do you think about the world situation?" a young boy asked.
The grandfather replied, "I feel like wolves are fighting in my heart.

One is full of anger and hatred; the other is full of love, forgiveness and peace.

"Which one will win?" asked the boy.

To which the grandfather replied, "The one you feed."

9. "Dealing with Difficult People"

Harvard Business School Press 2005

- Focus on behaviors rather than personalities.
- Confront situations before they get out of hand.
- Don't just do something — sit there. Sometimes doing nothing is the best answer.
- Instead of intervening, ask the person what they are going to do about the problem. This helps them to begin communicating in a more positive way.
- Sometimes "walking away" from a fight is the best thing to do.
- If you have a choice between being "right" or being "kind," choose kind.
- Understanding conflicting thinking styles.
  Synthesists have a desire to understand — they love to debate.
  Idealists want to reconcile differences of opinions.
  Pragmatists want concrete actions rather than analysis and theorizing.
  Analysts emphasize rational problem solving.
  Realists believe facts should be readily apparent to everyone.
  For instance, synthesists often conflict with pragmatists who want action and want to "get the job done."
- It is not just "what you say" but "how you say it" that counts.
- Always commit to being honest and telling the truth. This develops trust.
- Focus on desired changes in behavior for the future and set an action plan.

- Always give words of thanks and appreciation for positive behaviors.
- People who are angry, crabs, cranks and curmudgeons are just plain "pains and troublemakers."

Sometimes people may be in the wrong positions, not suited for them.

The book *Now, Discover Your Strengths* by Marcus Buckingham and Donald O. Clifton can test employees or board members for their strengths

There is also a book titled *Emotional Intelligence 2.0* by Travis Bradberry and Jean Greaves that tests a person's emotional strengths and weaknesses and has a test they can take and suggestions to improve. There are several versions of this book and the paperback and hardcover as well as the kindle that have different authors. I would recommend that you mention the author and which one has the test.

Daniel Goleman, another author of several emotional intelligence books, including *Emotional Intelligence: Why It Can Matter More Than IQ*, has the capacity for recognizing our own feelings and those of others by reading the room.

Intelligence is knowing what to say. Wisdom (emotional intelligence) is knowing whether to say it or not. Have a person signal another when they are being stubborn, inflexible or overreacting.

Difficult people are often low in self-awareness (How their behavior affects people.) Three hundred sixty evaluations of staff or board members where others' observations of behavior are made anonymously can be effective, not when used as performance evaluations but when used as a development process where a developmental coach sits down and goes over the feedback. This can be very powerful in motivating change in behavior. Emotional intelligence can be learned.

Soft skills, like self-awareness, self-regulation, empathy and social skills, can translate into hard results.

Harassment, anger management and employee grievances come up.

About 42% of a manager's time is spent dealing with conflict. It is better to have people work out conflicts among themselves. Collaboration and communication have to happen to solve these conflicts. Trust has to be developed.

Underperformers

Talk about it privately — never in front of a group. Producing is what matters.

Don't Avoid Conflicts, Manage Them

- There are people and institutional issues that will, if we let them, soak up our time and attention like a sponge. Ducking conflict may make it harder for us to achieve our goals.
- Premature decisions made before airing conflict often don't last. We should think of conflict as neither good nor bad — just the appearance of difference.
- We must probe for the underlying need or want from both sides.
- See the other person's positions and demands as valid.
- Take time to see where both sides have "common ground."
- In *Getting to Yes: Negotiating Agreement Without Giving In* by Roger Fisher, William L. Ury, Bruce Patton, it says to ask the other person's opinion first and then ask to tell your side of the story.
- Some conflicts dissolve with time.
- Define the problem as a person and you are in trouble. Define it as behavior and you can do something.

- Act promptly. When something negative is happening, interrupt the behavior and ask whether the conversation is working.
- As we shift from blaming people to solving problems, we create healthier organizations.
- The issue at the center of the argument can't be as important as the damage to relationships and self-esteem that might follow.
- A disagreement about an issue may be more about someone trying to establish a dominant position.

Always ask yourself whether it would matter to the organization if you won this difference of opinion. In the "big picture of life," how important is winning.

Phrases that can escalate conflict include:
   "How can you suggest that...?"
   "Anybody can see that..."
   "You can't be serious."

Phrases that are better:
   "Let me see if I understand your position..."
   "Maybe if we..."
   "I heard what you said — I want to see if I have it right."
- Be aware of non-verbal signs — eye rolling, leaning forward, fidgeting —sometimes calling a "time out"— then ask to tell your story and listen to the other person's story.
- You can't "unsay" what you have said — little misunderstandings can lead to "long-term grudges.
- Focus on the present to avoid the conflict – an agreement should be a shared vision of the future.

Negativity — People generally don't like change.
- How to have conversations that lead to action.
- You must have a vision to impart to your listener.
- Sometimes it takes a crisis to make people want to change behavior.

- People want to feel like they are part of something bigger than themselves.
- If you don't listen and respect employees, it's less likely they will listen to you.
- Always express appreciation.

10. 101 Zen Stories

By Nyogen Senzaki

What are the three secrets of happiness?

Once there was a middle-aged man who had fought his way up the corporate ladder. His marriage fell apart, he was estranged from his children, bored with his money and physically sick.

Then someone told him there was a wise man who knew the three secrets to a happy life.

The man quit his job, sold his home and began the quest to find the wise man with the secrets of happiness.

He found the wise man at last and knelt before him.

"Master," he said.
Please tell me the three secrets to a happy life.

The first secret to a happy life is to pay attention and be aware.

The man was delirious. He said he could most certainly do that.

What is the second secret to a happy life? The Zen Master replied,

To pay attention and be aware.

The man could barely believe his ears.
But the wise old man made it even clearer.

The third secret to a happy life is to pay attention and be aware.

Let us not look backwards in anger or forward in fear… but look around us with awareness.

11. "The Starfish Story"

Adapted from Loren Eisley

Once upon a time, there was a wise man who used to go to the ocean to do his writing. He had a habit of walking on the beach before he began his work.

One day, as he was walking along the shore, he looked down the beach and saw a human figure moving like a dancer. He smiled to himself at the thought of someone who would dance to the day, and so he walked faster to catch up.

As he got closer, he noticed that the figure was that of a young man, and that what he was doing was not dancing at all. The young man was reaching down to the shore, picking up small objects, and throwing them into the ocean.

He came closer still and called out, "Good morning! May I ask what it is that you are doing?"

The young man paused, looked up, and replied, "Throwing starfish into the ocean."

"I must ask, then, why are you throwing starfish into the ocean?" asked the somewhat startled wise man.

To this, the young man replied, "The sun is up and the tide is going out. If I don't throw them in, they'll die."

Upon hearing this, the wise man commented, "But, young man, do you not realize that there are miles and miles of beach and there are starfish all along every mile?
You can't possibly make a difference!"
At this, the young man bent down, picked up yet another starfish, and threw it into the ocean. As it met the water, he said, **"It made a difference for that one."**

There is something very special in each and everone of us.

We have all been gifted with the ability to make a difference.

If we can become aware of that gift we gain
through the strength of our visions, we will have
the power to change the future.

We must find our starfish.

We must find our starfish.

"Be the change you want to see in the world."

— *Mahatma Gandhi*

12. "Risks"

A poem by Janet Rand

To laugh is to risk appearing a fool,
To weep is to risk appearing sentimental.
To reach out to another is to risk involvement,
To expose feelings is to risk exposing your true self.

To place ideas and dreams before a crowd is to risk being called naive.
To love is to risk not being loved in return.
To live is to risk dying,

To hope is to risk despair.
To try is to risk failure.
But risk must be taken, because the greatest hazard
in life is to risk nothing.

The person who risks nothing, does nothing, has nothing,
is nothing, and becomes nothing.
They may avoid suffering and sorrow, but they
cannot learn, feel, change, grow, love, live.

Chained by their certitude, they are slaves, they have
forfeited their freedom.
Only a person who risks is truly free.

13. "What is Class?"

— A poem by Howard E. Ferguson author of *The Edge* https://www.perrymarshall. com/13894/what-is-class/

Class never runs scared. It is surefooted and confident in the knowledge that you can meet life head-on and handle whatever comes along. Those who have class have wrestled with their own personal "angel" and won a victory that marks them thereafter.

Class never makes excuses. It takes its lumps and learns from past mistakes.

Class is considerate of others. It knows that good manners are nothing more than a series of petty sacrifices.

Class bespeaks an aristocracy that has nothing to do with ancestors or money. The most affluent blueblood can be totally without class while the descendant of a Welsh miner may ooze class from every pore.

Class never tries to build itself up by tearing others down.

Class is already up and need not strive to look better by making others look worse.

Class can "walk with kings and keep its virtue, and talk with crowds and keep the common touch." Everyone is comfortable with the person who has class because they are comfortable with themselves.

If you have class, you don't need much of anything else.
If you don't have it, no matter what else you have — it doesn't make much difference.

14. COMMUNICATION

The ability to communicate with the most potent words expressed vividly and succinctly — simplicity trumps verbosity.

My 15 years as a science and honors chemistry teacher taught me excessive detail can confuse the listener. Your main point can be drowned by too much information.

When you are trying to make a point, precede it with a "pregnant pause" — use white space. Silence says a lot. Your audience will find the answers in the silence.

Your key sentence in every presentation is your first 15 words. They are as important as the next 1,500 words.

15. Speech Hints

Don't just make it brief — make it briefer.

Public Speaking:

- Tell people what you are going to tell them — tell them — then tell them what you have told them, meaning summarize it towards the end.
- Tell your stories in appropriate order.
- Empathy is immediate, instinctive and instantaneous. You pick up the signals others are sending if you have this talent.
- Because of our unique talents everyone sees the world a little differently.

16. Simplicity Is This

—By Steven Yellin

Grace comes with humility and humor comes with wisdom.
Keep it real, keep it simple, keep it humorous.
"Snackable bites" of information will be easily remembered.
Too many words just leave noise.
Levity, brevity, repetition make the best speeches.

When I coached high-school track, I would tell my runners to:
"Stay left and get back here as fast as you can."

17. "The Man Who Wins Is The Man Who Thinks He Can"

A poem by Walter D. Wintle

If you think you are beaten, you are
If you think you dare not, you don't,
If you like to win, but you think you can't
It's almost certain you won't.

If you think you'll lose, you've lost
For out in the world we find,
Success begins with a fellow's will
It's all in the state of mind.
If you think you are outclassed, you are
You've got to think high to rise,
You've got to be sure of yourself before
You can ever win a prize.

Life's battles don't always go
To the stronger or faster man,
But sooner or later the man who wins
Is the man who thinks he can!

18. "Don't Quit"

A poem by John Greenleaf Whittier

When things go wrong, as they sometimes will,
When the road you're trudging seems all uphill,
When the funds are low and the debt is high,
And you want to smile but you have to sigh,
When care is pressing you down a bit,
Rest if you must, but don't you quit.

Life is queer with its twists and turns,
As every one of us sometimes learns,
And many a person turns about
When they might have won had they stuck it out.
Don't give up though the pace seems slow —
You may succeed with another blow.

Often the goal is nearer than
It seems to a faint and a faltering man;
Often the struggler has given up
When he might have captured the victor's cup;
And they learned too late when the night came down,
How close he was to the golden crown.
Success is failure turned inside out —
The silver tint in the clouds of doubt,
And you can never tell how close you are,

It might become near when it seems afar;
So, stick to the fight when you're hardest hit —
It's when things seem worst that you must not quit.

19. "Persistence"

By President Calvin Coolidge

Nothing in the world can take the place of persistence.
Talent will not; nothing is more common than unsuccessful
men with talent.

Genius will not; unrewarded genius is almost a proverb.
Education will not; the world is full of educated derelicts.
Persistence and determination alone are omnipotent
The slogan "Press On" has solved and always will solve
the problems of the human race.

20. Rules for a Leader

- Walk the talk
- Keep it simple and keep it real
- Celebrate successes
- Know that courage matters
- Keep hope alive
- Take responsibility
- Develop a service attitude
- Aim for the heart
- Make a difference whenever and wherever you can
- If not us, then who?
- If not now, then when?
- It is never a wrong time to do the right thing
- When in doubt do the next right thing.

21. "Daring to Trust Again"

A leadership article by Newton Holt

Trust is the secret to speed to market, loyalty, responsiveness and a high-functioning, remarkable, organization.

Steven Covey's book *The Speed of Trust* has the potential to change everything.

1. High trust yields better financial performance.
2. Everything happens faster with trust. You can and will deliver what you say you are going to do.
3. Be careful not to overpromise and under-deliver.
4. To become a trusted leader you must show respect.
5. Not showing that one cares is a passive form of disrespect.
6. The most insidious form of disrespect is when a leader shows respect to some — to those who can do something for him or her — and not to others.
    You learn a lot about someone by the way he or she treats the waiter or waitress.
7. Another violation of respect is those who fake caring.
    If people do not think you care about them, they will withhold trust and not think you respect them and everything will take you longer and cost more.
8. Straight talk. Be honest and truthful to help build trust.
    False trust. One gives you the responsibility to get a job done but doesn't give you the authority or resources, or they "snoopervise" your activities.
9. Top leaders have both character and competence.

22. Persistence — My Story

In my life I was a teacher for 15 years.
I lost two babies before they were born because of tubal pregnancies.
I was devastated. Three months later... a miracle happened.
A woman showed up at the hospital where my husband, Bryan,
was doing his residency and wanted to give up her baby.
The baby was due the next day but was three weeks late.
So we took a risk. We blew caution to the wind, and we adopted
a brand new baby boy at three days.

We rose each time we fell.
Out of every tragedy in life there may be a triumph.
Climb Every Mountain!

The art of being wise is knowing what to overlook.
—*William James*

Suggested Additional Leadership Books

Now, Discover Your Strengths (Online test to determine your strengths)
By Marcus Buckingham & Donald O. Clifton

Emotional Intelligence 2.0 (Online tests to determine emotional intelligence) by Travis Bradberry and Jean Graves

The 21 Indispensable Qualities of a Leader: Becoming the Person Others Will Want to Follow
By John C. Maxwell

The 21 Irrefutable Laws of Leadership: Follow Them and People will Follow You
By John C. Maxwell

Emotional Intelligence: Why It Can Matter More Than IQ
By Daniel Goleman

The Simple Truths of Appreciation
By Barbara Glanz

7 Measures of Success: What Remarkable Associations Do That Others Don't
By the American Society of Association Executives (ASAE)

The Presentation Secrets of Steve Jobs: How to Be Insanely Great in Front of Any Audience
By Carmine Gallo

Crucial Conversations: Tools for Talking When the Stakes are High
By Joseph Grenny, Kerry Patterson, Ron McMillan & Al Switzler

Aim for the Heart: Leading to Build Great Teams
By Tom Mathews & Mac Anderson

The Essence of Leadership
By Mac Anderson

Rock Solid Leadership: How Great Leaders Exceed Expectations
By Robin Crow

Leading Change
By John P. Kotter

The Leadership Pill: The Missing Ingredient in Motivating People Today
By Kenneth Blanchard & Mark Muchnick

Influencer: The Power To Change Anything
By Kerry Patterson, Joseph Grenny, David Maxfield, Ron McMillan & Al Switzler

Purple Cow
By Seth Godin

Lincoln on Leadership: Executive Strategies for Tough Times
By Donald T. Phillips

The Art of Woo: Using Strategic Persuasion to Sell Your Ideas
By G. Richard Shell & Mario Moussa

The Truth About Getting the Best from People
By Martha I. Finney

Talent is Overrated: What Really Separates World-Class Performers from Everybody Else
By Geoff Colvin

Made to Stick: Why Some Ideas Survive and Others Die
By Chip Heath & Dan Heath

Our Iceberg is Melting: Changing and Succeeding Under Any Conditions
By John Kotter & Holger Rathgeber

Getting Together: Building Relationships As We Negotiate
By Roger Fisher & Scott Brown (Of The Harvard Negotiation Project)

The Speed of Trust: The One Thing That Changes Everything
By Stephen M. R. Covey

The 5 Levels of Leadership: Proven Steps To Maximize Your Potential
By John C. Maxwell

Principle Centered Leadership
By Stephen R. Covey

The 8th Habit: From Effectiveness to Greatness
By Steven R. Covey

Primal Leadership: Unleashing the Power of Emotional Intelligence
By Daniel Goleman

Built To Last: Successful Habits of Visionary Companies
By Jim Collins & Jerry I. Porras

How the Mighty Fall: And Why Some Companies Never Give In
By Jim Collins

Great By Choice
By Jim Collins & Morten T. Hansen

Anyway: The Paradoxical Commandments Finding Personal Meaning in a Crazy World
By Kent M. Keith & Spencer Johnson

The Truth About Negotiations
By Leigh Thompson

Talking to Strangers: What We Should Know About the People We Don't Know
By Malcom Gladwell

The Tipping Point: How Little Things Can Make a Big Difference
By Malcolm Gladwell

Outliers: The Story of Success
By Malcolm Gladwell

The Truth About Getting Your Point Across... And Nothing But The Truth
By Lonnie Pacelli

On Becoming a Leader
By Warren G. Bennis

Negotiating With Giants
By Peter D. Johnston

Getting to Yes: *Negotiating Agreement Without Giving In*
By Roger Fisher, William L. Ury & Bruce Patton

The Wisdom of Crowds: *Why The Many Are Smarter Than the Few And How Collective Wisdom Shapes Business, Economies, Societies and Nations*
By James Surowiecki & Grover Gardner

CPSIA information can be obtained
at www.ICGtesting.com
Printed in the USA
BVHW040342010623
665165BV00004B/11